Paul Breen

THE WILL TO DOUBT

The Will to Doubt

BY

BERTRAND RUSSELL

THE WISDOM LIBRARY

A DIVISION OF
PHILOSOPHICAL LIBRARY
New York

CONTENTS

THE WILL TO DOUBT

CAN MEN BE RATIONAL?

I am in the habit of thinking of myself as a Rationalist; and a Rationalist, I suppose, must be one who wishes men to be rational. But in these days rationality has received many hard knocks, so that it is difficult to know what one means by it, or whether, if that were known, it is something which human beings can achieve. The question of the definition of rationality has two sides, theoretical and practical: what is a rational opinion? and what is rational conduct? Pragmatism emphasizes the irrationality of opinion, and psycho-analysis emphasizes the irrationality of conduct. Both have led many people to the view that there is no such thing as an ideal rationality to which opinion and conduct might with advantage conform. It would seem to follow that, if you and I hold different opinions, it is useless to appeal to argument, or to seek the arbitrament of an impartial outsider; there is nothing for us to do but fight it out, by the methods of rhetoric, advertisement, or warfare, according to the degree of our financial and military strength. I believe such an outlook to be very dangerous, and in the long run, fatal to civilization. I shall, therefore, endeavour to show that the ideal of rationality remains unaffected by the ideas that have been thought fatal to it, and that it retains all the importance it was formerly believed to have as a guide to thought and life.

To begin with rationality in opinion: I should define

it merely as the habit of taking account of all relevant evidence in arriving at a belief. Where certainty is unattainable, a rational man will give most weight to the most probable opinion, while retaining others, which have an appreciable probability, in his mind as hypotheses which subsequent evidence may show to be preferable. This, of course, assumes that it is possible in many cases to ascertain facts and probabilities by an objective method—i.e., a method which will lead any two careful people to the same result. This is often questioned. It is said by many that the only function of intellect is to facilitate the satisfaction of the individual's desires and needs. The Plebs Text-Books Committee, in their *Outline of Psychology* (p. 68), say: "*The intellect is above all things an instrument of partiality. Its function is to secure that those actions which are beneficial to the individual or the species shall be performed, and that those actions which are less beneficial shall be inhibited.*" (Italics in the original.)

But the same authors, in the same book (p. 123), state, again in italics: "*The faith of the Marxian differs profoundly from religious faith: the latter is based only on desire and tradition; the former is grounded on the scientific analysis of objective reality.*" This seems inconsistent with what they say about the intellect, unless, indeed, they mean to suggest that it is not intellect which has led them to adopt the Marxian faith. In any case, since they admit that "scientific analysis of objective reality" is possible, they must admit that it is possible to have opinions which are rational in an objective sense.

More erudite authors who advocate an irrationalist point of view, such as the pragmatist philosophers, are not to be caught out so easily. They maintain that there is no such thing as objective fact to which our opinions must conform if they are to be true. For them opinions are merely weapons in the struggle for existence, and those which help a man to survive are to be called "true." This view was prevalent in Japan in the sixth century A.D., when Buddhism first reached that country. The Government, being in doubt as to the truth of the new religion, ordered one of the courtiers to adopt it experimentally; if he prospered more than the others, the religion was to be adopted universally. This is the method (with modifications to suit modern times) which the pragmatists advocate in regard to all religious controversies.

In spite of the pragmatist's definition of "truth," however, he has always, in ordinary life, a quite different standard for the less refined questions which arise in practical affairs. A pragmatist on a jury in a murder case will weigh the evidence exactly as any other man will, whereas if he adopted his professed criterion he ought to consider whom among the population it would be most profitable to hang. That man would be, by definition, guilty of the murder, since belief in his guilt would be more useful, and therefore more "true," than belief in the guilt of anyone else. I am afraid such practical pragmatism does sometimes occur; I have heard of "frame-ups" in Russia which answered to this description. But in such cases all possible efforts after concealment are made, and if they fail there is a scandal. This effort after concealment shows that even policemen believe in objective truth in the case of a criminal trial. It is this kind of objective truth—a very mundane and pedestrian affair—that is sought in science. It is this kind also that is sought in religion so long as people hope to find it. It is only when people have given up the hope of proving that religion is true in a straightforward sense that they set to work to prove that it is "true" in some newfangled sense. It may be laid down broadly that irrationalism, i.e. disbelief in objective fact, arises almost always from the desire to assert something for which there is no evidence, or to deny something for which there is very good evidence. But the belief in objective fact always persists as regards particular practical questions, such as investments or engaging servants. And if fact can be made the test of the truth of our beliefs anywhere, it should be the test everywhere, leading to agnosticism wherever it cannot be applied.

The above considerations are, of course, very inadequate to their theme. The question of the objectivity of fact has been rendered difficult by the obfuscations of philosophers, with which I have attempted to deal elsewhere in a more thoroughgoing fashion. For the present I shall assume that there are facts, that some facts can be known, and that in regard to certain others a degree of probability can be ascertained in relation to facts which can be known. Our beliefs are, however, often contrary to fact; even when we only hold that something is probable on the evidence, it may be that we ought to hold it to be improbable on the same evidence. The theoretical part of rationality, then, will consist in basing our beliefs as regards matters of fact upon evidence rather than upon wishes, prejudices, or traditions. According to the subject-matter, a rational man will be the same as one who is judicial or one who is scientific.

There are some who think that psycho-analysis has shown the impossibility of being rational in our beliefs, by pointing out the strange and almost lunatic origin of many people's cherished convictions. I have a very high respect for psycho-analysis, and I believe that it can be enormously useful. But the popular mind has somewhat lost sight of the purpose which has mainly inspired Freud and his followers. Their method is primarily one of therapeutics, a way of curing hysteria and various kinds of insanity. During the war psycho-analysis proved to be far the most potent treatment for war-neuroses. Rivers's *Instinct and the Unconscious,* which is largely based upon experience of "shell-shock" patients, gives a beautiful analysis of the morbid effects of fear when it cannot be straightforwardly indulged. These effects, of course, are largely non-intellectual; they include various kinds of paralysis, and all sorts of apparently physical ailments. With these, for the moment, we are not concerned; it is intellectual derangements that form our theme. It is found that many of the delusions of lunatics result from instinctive obstructions, and can be cured by purely mental means—i.e. by making the patient bring to mind facts of which he had repressed the memory. This kind of treatment, and the outlook which inspires it, pre-suppose an ideal of sanity, from which the patient has departed, and to which he is to be brought back by making him conscious of all the relevant facts, including those which he most wishes to forget. This is the exact opposite of that lazy acquiescence in irrationality which is sometimes urged by those who only know that psychoanalysis has shown the prevalence of irrational beliefs, and who forget or ignore that its purpose is to diminish this prevalence by a definite method of medical treatment. A closely similar method can cure the irrationalities of those who are not recognized lunatics, provided they will submit to treatment by a practitioner free from their delusions. Presidents, Cabinet Ministers, and Eminent Persons, however, seldom fulfil this condition, and therefore remain uncured.

So far, we have been considering only the theoretical side of rationality. The practical side, to which we must now turn our attention, is more difficult. Differences of opinion on practical questions spring from two sources: first, differences between the desires of the disputants; secondly, differences in their estimates of the means of realizing their desires. Differences of the second kind are really theoretical, and only derivatively practical. For example, some authorities hold that our first line of defence should consist of battleships, others that it should consist of aeroplanes. Here there is no difference as regards the end proposed, namely, national defence, but only as to the means. The argument can therefore be conducted in a purely scientific manner, since the disagreement which causes the dispute is only as to facts, present or future, certain or probable. To all such cases the kind of rationality which I called theoretical applies, in spite of the fact that a practical issue is involved.

There is, however, in many cases which appear to come under this head a complication which is very important in practice. A man who desires to act in a certain way will persuade himself that by so acting he will achieve some end which he considers good, even when, if he had no such desire, he would see no reason for such a belief. And he will judge quite differently as to matters of fact and as to probabilities from the way in which a man with contrary desires will judge. Gamblers, as every one knows, are full of irrational beliefs as to systems which *must* lead them to win in the long run. People who take an interest in politics persuade themselves that the leaders of their party would never be guilty of the knavish tricks practiced by opposing politicians. Men who like administration think that it is good for the populace to be treated like a herd of sheep, men who like tobacco say that it soothes the nerves, and men who like alcohol say that it stimulates wit. The bias produced by such causes falsifies men's judgments as to facts in a way which is very hard to avoid. Even a learned scientific article about the effects of alcohol on the nervous system will generally betray by internal evidence whether the author is or not a teetotaller; in either case he has a tendency to see the facts in the way that would justify his own practice. In politics and religion such considerations become very important. Most men think that in framing their political opinions they are actuated by desire for the public good; but nine times out of ten a man's politics can be predicted from the way in which he makes his living. This has led some people to maintain, and many more to believe practically, that in such matters it is impossible to be objective, and that no method is possible except a tug-of-war between classes with opposite bias.

It is just in such matters, however, that psycho-analysis is particularly useful, since it enables men to become aware of a bias which has hitherto been unconscious. It gives a technique for seeing ourselves as others see us, and a reason for supposing that this view of ourselves is less unjust than we are inclined to think. Combined with a training in the scientific outlook, this method could, if it were widely taught, enable people to be infinitely more rational than they are at present as regards all their beliefs about matters of fact, and about the probable effect of any proposed action. And if men did not disagree about such matters, the disagreements which might survive would almost certainly be found capable of amicable adjustment.

There remains, however, a residuum which cannot be treated by purely intellectual methods. The desires of one man do not by any means harmonize completely with those of another. Two competitors on the Stock Exchange might be in complete agreement as to what would be the effect of this or that action, but this would not produce practical harmony, since each wishes to grow rich at the expense of the other. Yet even here rationality is capable of preventing most of the harm that might otherwise occur. We call a man irrational when he acts in a passion, when he cuts off his nose to spite his face. He is irrational because he forgets that, by indulging the desire which he happens to feel most strongly at the moment, he will thwart other desires which in the long run are more important to him. If men were rational, they would take a more correct view of their own interest than they do at present; and if all men acted from enlightened self-interest the world would be a paradise in comparison with what it is. I do not maintain that there is nothing better than self-interest as a motive to action; but I do maintain that self-interest, like altruism, is better when it is enlightened than when it is unenlightened. In an ordered community it is very rarely to a man's interest to do anything which is very harmful to others. The less rational a man is, the oftener he will fail to perceive how what injures others also injures him, because hatred or envy will blind him. Therefore, although I do not pretend that enlightened self-interest is the highest morality, I do maintain that, if it became common, it would make the world an immeasurably better place than it is.

Rationality in practice may be defined as the habit of remembering all our relevant desires, and not only the one which happens at the moment to be strongest. Like rationality in opinion, it is a matter of degree. Complete rationality is no doubt an unattainable ideal, but so long as we continue to classify some men as lunatics it is clear that we think some men more rational than others. I believe that all solid progress in the world consists of an increase in rationality, both practical and theoretical. To preach an altruistic morality appears to me somewhat useless, because it will appeal only to those who already have altruistic desires. But to preach rationality is somewhat different, since rationality helps us to realize our own desires on the whole, whatever they may be. A man is rational in proportion as his intelligence informs and controls his desires. I believe that the control of our acts by our intelligence is ultimately what is of most importance, and what alone will make social life remain possible as science increases the means at our disposal for injuring each other. Education, the press, politics, religion—in a word, all the great forces in the world—are at present on the side of irrationality; they are in the hands of men who flatter King Demos in order to lead him astray. The remedy does not lie in anything heroically cataclysmic, but in the efforts of individuals towards a more sane and balanced view of our relations to our neighbours and to the world. It is to intelligence, increasingly widespread, that we must look for the solution of the ills from which our world is suffering.

FREE THOUGHT AND OFFICIAL PROPAGANDA

Moncure Conway devoted his life to two great objects: freedom of thought, and freedom of the individual. In regard to both these objects, something has been gained since his time, but something also has been lost. New dangers, somewhat different in form from those of past ages, threaten both kinds of freedom, and unless a vigorous and vigilant public opinion can be aroused in defence of them, there will be much less of both a hundred years hence than there is now.

Let us begin by trying to be clear as to what we mean by "free thought." This expression has two senses. In its narrower sense it means thought which does not accept the dogmas of traditional religion. In this sense a man is a "free thinker" if he is not a Christian or a Mussulman or a Buddhist or a Shintoist or a member of any of the other bodies of men who accept some inherited orthodoxy. In Christian countries a man is called a "free thinker" if he does not decidedly believe in God, though this would not suffice to make a man a "free thinker" in a Buddhist country.

I do not wish to minimize the importance of free thought in this sense. I am myself a dissenter from all known religions, and I hope that every kind of religious belief will die out. I do not believe that, on the balance, religious belief has been a force for good. Although I am prepared to admit that in certain times and places it has had some good effects, I regard it as belonging to the infancy of human reason, and to a stage of development which we are now outgrowing.

But there is also a wider sense of "free thought," which I regard as of still greater importance. Indeed, the harm done by traditional religions seems chiefly traceable to the fact that they have prevented free thought in this wider sense. The wider sense is not so easy to define as the narrower, and it will be well to spend some little time in trying to arrive at its essence.

When we speak of anything as "free," our meaning is not definite unless we can say what it is free *from*. Whatever or whoever is "free" is not subject to some external compulsion, and to be precise we ought to say what this kind of compulsion is. Thus thought is "free" when it is free from certain kinds of outward control which are often present. Some of these kinds of control which must be absent if thought is to be "free" are obvious, but others are more subtle and elusive.

To begin with the most obvious. Thought is not "free" when legal penalties are incurred by the holding or not holding of certain opinions, or by giving expression to one's belief or lack of belief on certain matters. Very few countries in the world have as yet even this elementary kind of freedom. In England, under the Blasphemy Laws, it is illegal to express disbelief in the Christian religion, though in practice the law is not set in motion against the well-to-do. It is also illegal to teach what Christ taught on the subject of non-resistance. Therefore, whoever wishes to avoid becoming a criminal must profess to agree with Christ's teaching, but must avoid saying what that teaching was. In America no one can enter the country without first solemnly declaring that he disbelieves in anarchism and polygamy; and, once inside, he must also disbelieve in communism. In Japan it is illegal to express disbelief in the divinity of the Mikado. It will thus be seen that a voyage round the world is a perilous adventure. A Mohammedan, a Tolstoyan, a Bolshevik, or a Christian cannot undertake it without at some point becoming a criminal, or holding his tongue about what he considers important truths. This, of course, applies only to steerage passengers; saloon passengers are allowed to believe whatever they please, provided they avoid offensive obtrusiveness.

It is clear that the most elementary condition, if thought is to be free, is the absence of legal penalties for the expression of opinions. No great country has yet reached to this level, although most of them think they have. The opinions which are still persecuted strike the majority as so monstrous and immoral that the general principle of toleration cannot be held to apply to them. But this is exactly the same view as that which made possible the tortures of the Inquisition. There was a time when Protestantism seemed as wicked as Bolshevism seems now. Please do not infer from this remark that I am either a Protestant or a Bolshevik.

Legal penalties are, however, in the modern world, the least of the obstacles to freedom of thought. The two great obstacles are economic penalties and distortion of evidence. It is clear that thought is not free if the profession of certain opinions makes it impossible to earn a living. It is clear also that thought is not free if all the arguments on one side of a controversy are perpetually presented as attractively as possible, while the arguments on the other side can only be discovered by diligent search. Both these obstacles exist in every large country known to me, except China, which is the last refuge of freedom. It is these obstacles with which I shall be concerned—their present magnitude, the likelihood of their increase, and the possibility of their diminution.

We may say that thought is free when it is exposed to free competition among beliefs—i.e., when all beliefs are able to state their case, and no legal or pecuniary advantages or disadvantages attach to beliefs. This is an ideal which, for various reasons, can never be fully attained. But it is possible to approach very much nearer to it than we do at present.

Three incidents in my own life will serve to show how, in modern England, the scales are weighted in favour of Christianity. My reason for mentioning them is that many people do not at all realize the disadvantages to which avowed Agnosticism still exposes people.

The first incident belongs to a very early stage in my life. My father was a Freethinker, but died when I was only three years old. Wishing me to be brought up without superstition, he appointed two Freethinkers as my guardians. The Courts, however, set aside his will, and had me educated in the Christian faith. I am afraid the result was disappointing, but that was not the fault of the law. If he had directed that I should be educated as a Christadelphian or a Muggletonian or a Seventh-day Adventist, the Courts would not have dreamed of objecting. A parent has a right to ordain that any imaginable superstition shall be instilled into his children after his death, but has not the right to say that they shall be kept free from superstition if possible.

The second incident occurred in the year 1910. I had at that time a desire to stand for Parliament as a Liberal, and the Whigs recommended me to a certain constituency. I addressed the Liberal Association, who expressed themselves favourably, and my adoption seemed certain. But, on being questioned by a small inner caucus, I admitted that I was an Agnostic. They asked whether the fact would come out, and I said it probably would. They asked whether I should be willing to go to church occasionally, and I replied that I should not. Consequently, they selected another candidate, who was duly elected, has been in Parliament ever since, and is a member of the present Government.

The third incident occurred immediately afterwards. I was invited by Trinity College, Cambridge, to become a lecturer, but not a Fellow. The difference is not pecuniary; it is that a Fellow has a vote in the government of the College, and cannot be dispossessed during the term of his Fellowship except for grave immorality. The chief reason for not offering me a Fellowship was that the clerical party did not wish to add to the anti-clerical vote. The result was that they were able to dismiss me in 1916, when they disliked my views on the war.* If I had been dependent on my lectureship, I should have starved.

These three incidents illustrate different kinds of disadvantages attaching to avowed freethinking even in modern England. Any other avowed Freethinker could supply similar incidents from his personal experience, often of a far more serious character. The net result is that people who are not well-to-do dare not be frank about their religious beliefs.

It is not, of course, only or even chiefly in regard to religion that there is lack of freedom. Belief in communism or free love handicaps a man much more than Agnosticism. Not only is it a disadvantage to hold those views, but it is very much more difficult to obtain publicity for the arguments in their favour. On the other hand, in Russia the advantages and disadvantages are exactly reversed: comfort and power are achieved by professing Atheism, communism, and free love, and no opportunity exists for propaganda against these opinions. The result is that in Russia one set of fanatics feels absolute certainty about one set of doubtful propositions, while in the rest of the world another set of fanatics feels equal certainty about a diametrically opposite set of equally doubtful propositions. From such a situation war, bitterness, and persecution inevitably result on both sides.

William James used to preach the "will to believe." For my part, I should wish to preach the "will to doubt." None of our beliefs are quite true; all have at least a penumbra of vagueness and error. The methods

* I should add that they re-appointed me later, when war passions had begun to cool.

of increasing the degree of truth in our beliefs are well known; they consist in hearing all sides, trying to ascertain all the relevant facts, controlling our own bias by discussion with people who have the opposite bias, and cultivating a readiness to discard any hypothesis which has proved inadequate. These methods are practised in science, and have built up the body of scientific knowledge. Every man of science whose outlook is truly scientific is ready to admit that what passes for scientific knowledge at the moment is sure to require correction with the progress of discovery; nevertheless, it is near enough to the truth to serve for most practical purposes, though not for all. In science, where alone something approximating to genuine knowledge is to be found, men's attitude is tentative and full of doubt.

In religion and politics, on the contrary, though there is as yet nothing approaching scientific knowledge, everybody considers it *de rigueur* to have a dogmatic opinion, to be backed up by inflicting starvation, prison, and war, and to be carefully guarded from argumentative competition with any different opinion. If only men could be brought into a tentatively agnostic frame of mind about these matters, nine-tenths of the evils of the modern world would be cured. War would become impossible, because each side would realize that both sides must be in the wrong. Persecution would cease. Education would aim at expanding the mind, not at narrowing it. Men would be chosen for jobs on account of fitness to do the work, not because they flattered the irrational dogmas of those in power. Thus rational doubt alone, if it could be generated, would suffice to introduce the millennium.

We have had in recent years a brilliant example of the scientific temper of mind in the theory of relativity and its reception by the world. Einstein, a German-Swiss-Jew pacifist, was appointed to a research professorship by the German Government in the early days of the 1914-18 war; his predictions were verified by an English expedition which observed the eclipse of 1919, very soon after the Armistice. This theory upsets the whole theoretical framework of traditional physics; it is almost as damaging to orthodox dynamics as Darwin was to *Genesis*. Yet physicists everywhere have shown complete readiness to accept his theory as soon as it appeared that the evidence was in its favour. But none of them, least of all Einstein himself, would claim that he has said the last word. He has not built a monument of infallible dogma to stand for all time. There are difficulties he cannot solve; his doctrines will have to be modified in their turn as they have modified Newton's. This critical undogmatic receptiveness is the true attitude of science.

What would have happened if Einstein had advanced something equally new in the sphere of religion or politics? English people would have found elements of Prussianism in his theory; anti-Semites would have regarded it as a Zionist plot; nationalists in all countries would have found it tainted with lily-livered pacifism, and proclaimed it a mere dodge for escaping military service. All the old-fashioned professors would have approached Scotland Yard to get the importation of his writings prohibited. Teachers favourable to him would have been dismissed. He, meantime, would have captured the Government of some backward country, where it would have become illegal to teach anything except his doctrine, which would have grown into a mysterious dogma not understood by anybody. Ultimately the truth or falsehood of his doctrine would be decided on the battlefield, without the collection of any fresh evidence for or against it. This method is the logical outcome of William James's will to believe.

What is wanted is not the will to believe, but the wish to find out, which is its exact opposite.

If it is admitted that a condition of rational doubt would be desirable, it becomes important to inquire how it comes about that there is so much irrational certainty in the world. A great deal of this is due to the inherent irrationality and credulity of average human nature. But this seed of intellectual original sin is nourished and fostered by other agencies, among which three play the chief part—namely, education, propaganda, and economic pressure. Let us consider these in turn.

(1) *Education.*—Elementary education, in all advanced countries, is in the hands of the State. Some of the things taught are known to be false by the officials who prescribe them, and many others are known to be false, or at any rate very doubtful, by every unprejudiced person. Take, for example, the teaching of history. Each nation aims only at self-glorification in the school text-books of history. When a man writes his autobiography he is expected to show a certain modesty; but when a nation writes its autobiography there is no limit to its boasting and vainglory. When I was young, school books taught that the French were wicked and the Germans virtuous; now they teach the opposite. In neither case is there the slightest regard for truth. German school books, dealing with the battle of Waterloo, represent Wellington as all but defeated when Blücher saved the situation; English books represent Blücher as having made very little difference. The writers of both the German and the English books know that they are not telling the truth. American school books used to be violently anti-British; since the war of 1914-18 they have become equally pro-British, without aiming at truth in either case (see *The Freeman*, Feb. 15, 1922, p. 523). Both before and since, one of the chief purposes of education in the United States has been to turn the motley collection of immigrant children into "good Americans." Apparently it has not occurred to any one that a "good American," like a "good German" or a "good Japanese," must be, *pro tanto*, a bad human being. A "good American" is a man or woman imbued with the belief that America is the finest country on earth, and ought always to be enthusiastically supported in any quarrel. It is just possible that these propositions are true; if

so, a rational man will have no quarrel with them. But if they are true, they ought to be taught everywhere, not only in America. It is a suspicious circumstance that such propositions are never believed outside the particular country which they glorify. Meanwhile the whole machinery of the State, in all the different countries, is turned on to making defenseless children believe absurd propositions the effect of which is to make them willing to die in defence of sinister interests under the impression that they are fighting for truth and right. This is only one of countless ways in which education is designed, not to give true knowledge, but to make the people pliable to the will of their masters. Without an elaborate system of deceit in the elementary schools it would be impossible to preserve the camouflage of democracy.

Before leaving the subject of education, I will take another example from America*—not because America is any worse than other countries, but because it is the most modern—showing the dangers that are growing rather than those that are diminishing. In the State of New York a school cannot be established without a license from the State, even if it is to be supported wholly by private funds. A recent law decrees that a license shall not be granted to any school "where it shall appear that the instruction proposed to be given includes the teaching of the doctrine that organized Governments shall be overthrown by force, violence, or unlawful means." As *The New Republic* points out, there is no limitation to this or that organized Government. The law therefore would have made it illegal, during the last war, to teach the doctrine that the Kaiser's Government should be overthrown by force; and, since then, the support of Kolchak or Denikin against the Soviet Government would have been illegal. Such consequences, of course, were not intended, and result only from bad draughtsmanship. What was in-

* See *The New Republic*, Feb. 1, 1922, pp. 259 ff.

tended appears from another law passed at the same time, applying to teachers in State schools. This law provides that certificates permitting persons to teach in such schools shall be issued only to those who have "shown satisfactorily" that they are "loyal and obedient to the Government of this State and of the United States," and shall be refused to those who have advocated, no matter where or when, "a form of government other than the Government of this State or of the United States." The committee which framed these laws, as quoted by *The New Republic*, laid it down that the teacher who "does not approve of the present social system . . . must surrender his office," and that "no person who is not eager to combat the theories of social change should be entrusted with the task of fitting the young and old for the responsibilities of citizenship." Thus, according to the law of the State of New York, Christ and George Washington were too degraded morally to be fit for the education of the young. If Christ were to go to New York and say, "Suffer the little children to come unto me," the President of the New York School Board would reply: "Sir, I see no evidence that you are eager to combat theories of social change. Indeed, I have heard it said that you advocate what you call the *kingdom* of heaven, whereas this country, thank God, is a republic. It is clear that the Government of your kingdom of heaven would differ materially from that of New York State, therefore no children will be allowed access to you." If he failed to make this reply, he would not be doing his duty as a functionary entrusted with the administration of the law.

The effect of such laws is very serious. Let it be granted, for the sake of argument, that the government and the social system in the State of New York are the best that have ever existed on this planet; yet even then both would presumably be capable of improvement. Any person who admits this obvious proposition is by law incapable of teaching in a State school. Thus the law decrees that the teachers shall all be either hypocrites or fools.

The growing danger exemplified by the New York law is that resulting from the monopoly of power in the hands of a single organization, whether the State or a Trust or federation of Trusts. In the case of education, the power is in the hands of the State, which can prevent the young from hearing of any doctrine which it dislikes. I believe there are still some people who think that a democratic State is scarcely distinguishable from the people. This, however, is a delusion. The State is a collection of officials, different for different purposes, drawing comfortable incomes so long as the *status quo* is preserved. The only alteration they are likely to desire in the *status quo* is an increase of bureaucracy and of the power of bureaucrats. It is, therefore, natural that they should take advantage of such opportunities as war excitement to acquire inquisitorial powers over their employees, involving the right to inflict starvation upon any subordinate who opposes them. In matters of the mind, such as education, this state of affairs is fatal. It puts an end to all possibility of progress or freedom or intellectual initiative. Yet it is the natural result of allowing the whole of elementary education to fall under the sway of a single organization.

Religious toleration, to a certain extent, has been won because people have ceased to consider religion so important as it was once thought to be. But in politics and economics, which have taken the place formerly occupied by religion, there is a growing tendency to persecution, which is not by any means confined to one party. The persecution of opinion in Russia is more severe than in any capitalist country. I met in Petrograd an eminent Russian poet, Alexander Block, who has since died as the result of privations. The Bolsheviks allowed him to teach æsthetics, but he complained that they insisted on his teaching the subject "from a Marxian point of view." He had been at a loss to discover how the theory of rhythmics was connected with Marxism, although, to avoid starvation, he had done his best to find out. Of course, it has been impossible in Russia ever since the Bolsheviks came to power to print anything critical of the dogmas upon which their regime is founded.

The example of Russia illustrates the conclusion to which we seem to be driven—namely, that so long as men continue to have the present fanatical belief in the importance of politics, free thought on political matters will be impossible, and there is only too much danger that the lack of freedom will spread to all other matters, as it has done in Russia. Only some degree of political scepticism can save us from this misfortune.

It must not be supposed that the officials in charge of education desire the young to become educated. On the contrary, their problem is to impart information without imparting intelligence. Education should have two objects: first, to give definite knowledge—reading and writing, languages and mathematics, and so on; secondly, to create those mental habits which will enable people to acquire knowledge and form sound judgments for themselves. The first of these we may call information, the second intelligence. The utility of information is admitted practically as well as theoretically; without a literate population a modern State is impossible. But the utility of intelligence is admitted only theoretically, not practically; it is not desired that ordinary people should think for themselves, because it is felt that people who think for themselves are awkward to manage and cause administrative difficulties. Only the guardians, in Plato's language, are to think; the rest are to obey, or to follow leaders like a herd of sheep. This doctrine, often unconsciously, has survived the introduction of political democracy, and has radically vitiated all national systems of education.

The country which has succeeded best in giving information without intelligence is the latest addition to modern civilization, Japan. Elementary education in

Japan is said to be admirable from the point of view of instruction. But, in addition to instruction, it has another purpose, which is to teach worship of the Mikado—a far stronger creed now than before Japan became modernized.* Thus the schools have been used simultaneously to confer knowledge and to promote superstition. Since we are not tempted to Mikado-worship, we see clearly what is absurd in Japanese teaching. Our own national superstitions strike us as natural and sensible, so that we do not take such a true view of them as we do of the superstitions of Nippon. But if a travelled Japanese were to maintain the thesis that our schools teach superstitions just as inimical to intelligence as belief in the divinity of the Mikado, I suspect that he would be able to make out a very good case.

For the present I am not in search of remedies, but am only concerned with diagnosis. We are faced with the paradoxical fact that education has become one of the chief obstacles to intelligence and freedom of thought. This is due primarily to the fact that the State claims a monopoly; but that is by no means the sole cause.

(2) *Propaganda.*—Our system of education turns young people out of the schools able to read, but for the most part unable to weigh evidence or to form an independent opinion. They are then assailed, throughout the rest of their lives, by statements designed to make them believe all sorts of absurd propositions, such as that Blank's pills cure all ills, that Spitzbergen is warm and fertile, and that Germans eat corpses. The art of propaganda, as practised by modern politicians and governments, is derived from the art of advertisement. The science of psychology owes a great deal to advertisers. In former days most psychologists would probably have thought that a man could not convince

* See The Invention of a New Religion. By Professor Chamberlain, of Tokyo. Published by the Rationalist Press Association. (Now out of print.)

many people of the excellence of his own wares by merely stating emphatically that they were excellent. Experience shows, however, that they were mistaken in this. If I were to stand up once in a public place and state that I am the most modest man alive, I should be laughed at; but if I could raise enough money to make the same statement on all the buses and on hoardings along all the principal railway lines, people would presently become convinced that I had an abnormal shrinking from publicity. If I were to go to a small shopkeeper and say: "Look at your competitor over the way, he is getting your business; don't you think it would be a good plan to leave your business and stand up in the middle of the road and try to shoot him before he shoots you?"—if I were to say this, any small shopkeeper would think me mad. But when the Government says it with emphasis and a brass band, the small shopkeepers become enthusiastic, and quite surprised when they find afterwards that business has suffered. Propaganda, conducted by the means which advertisers have found successful, is now one of the recognized methods of government in all advanced countries, and is especially the method by which democratic opinion is created.

There are two different evils about propaganda as now practised. On the one hand, its appeal is generally to irrational causes of belief rather than to serious argument; on the other hand, it gives an unfair advantage to those who can obtain most publicity, whether through wealth or through power. For my part, I am inclined to think that too much fuss is sometimes made about the fact that propaganda appeals to emotion rather than reason. The line between emotion and reason is not so sharp as some people think. Moreover, a clever man could frame a sufficiently rational argument in favour of any position which has any chance of being adopted. There are always good arguments on both sides of any real issue. Definite mis-statements of fact can be legitimately objected to, but they are by no means necessary. The mere words "Pear's Soap," which affirm nothing, cause people to buy that article. If, wherever these words appear, they were replaced by the words "The Labour Party," millions of people would be led to vote for the Labour Party, although the advertisements had claimed no merit for it whatever. But if both sides in a controversy were confined by law to statements which a committee of eminent logicians considered relevant and valid, the main evil of propaganda, as at present conducted, would remain. Suppose, under such a law, two parties with an equally good case, one of whom had a million pounds to spend on propaganda, while the other had only a hundred thousand. It is obvious that the arguments in favour of the richer party would become more widely known than those in favour of the poorer party, and therefore the richer party would win. This situation is, of course, intensified when one party is the Government. In Russia the Government has an almost complete monopoly of propaganda, but that is not necessary. The advantages which it possesses over its opponents will generally be sufficient to give it the victory, unless it has an exceptionally bad case.

The objection to propaganda is not only its appeal to unreason, but still more the unfair advantage which it gives to the rich and powerful. Equality of opportunity among opinions is essential if there is to be real freedom of thought; and equality of opportunity among opinions can only be secured by elaborate laws directed to that end, which there is no reason to expect to see enacted. The cure is not to be sought primarily in such laws, but in better education and a more sceptical public opinion. For the moment, however, I am not concerned to discuss cures.

(3) *Economic pressure.*—I have already dealt with some aspects of this obstacle to freedom of thought, but I wish now to deal with it on more general lines, as a danger which is bound to increase unless very definite steps are taken to counteract it. The supreme

example of economic pressure applied against freedom of thought is Soviet Russia, where, until the trade agreement, the Government could and did inflict starvation upon people whose opinions it disliked— for example, Kropotkin. But in this respect Russia is only somewhat ahead of other countries. In France, during the Dreyfus affair, any teacher would have lost his position if he had been in favour of Dreyfus at the start or against him at the end. In America at the present day I doubt if a university professor, however eminent, could get employment if he were to criticize the Standard Oil Company, because all college presidents have received or hope to receive benefactions from Mr. Rockefeller. Throughout America Socialists are marked men, and find it extremely difficult to obtain work unless they have great gifts. The tendency, which exists wherever industrialism is well developed, for trusts and monopolies to control all industry, leads to a diminution of the number of possible employers, so that it becomes easier and easier to keep secret black books by means of which any one not subservient to the great corporations can be starved. The growth of monopolies is introducing in America many of the evils associated with State Socialism as it has existed in Russia. From the standpoint of liberty, it makes no difference to a man whether his only possible employer is the State or a Trust.

In America, which is the most advanced country industrially, and to a lesser extent in other countries which are approximating to the American condition, it is necessary for the average citizen, if he wishes to make a living, to avoid incurring the hostility of certain big men. And these big men have an outlook—religious, moral, and political—with which they expect their employees to agree, at least outwardly. A man who openly dissents from Christianity, or believes in a relaxation of the marriage laws, or objects to the power of the great corporations, finds America a very uncomfortable country, unless he happens to be an eminent writer. Exactly the same kind of restraints upon freedom of thought are bound to occur in every country where economic organization has been carried to the point of practical monopoly. Therefore the safeguarding of liberty in the world which is growing up is far more difficult than it was in the nineteenth century, when free competition was still a reality. Whoever are about the freedom of the mind must face this uation fully and frankly, realizing the inapplicability methods which answered well enough while industrialism was in its infancy.

There are two simple principles which, if they were dopted, would solve almost all social problems. The first is that education should have for one of its aims to teach people only to believe propositions when there is some reason to think that they are true. The second is that jobs should be given solely for fitness to do the work.

To take the second point first. The habit of considering a man's religious, moral, and political opinions before appointing him to a post or giving him a job is the modern form of persecution, and it is likely to become quite as efficient as the Inquisition ever was. The old liberties can be legally retained without being of the slightest use. If, in practice, certain opinions lead a man to starve, it is poor comfort to him to know that his opinions are not punishable by law. There is certain public feeling against starving men for not belonging to the Church of England, or for holding ightly unorthodox opinions in politics. But there is hardly any feeling against the rejection of Atheists or Mormons, extreme communists, or men who advocate ree love. Such men are thought to be wicked, and it is considered only natural to refuse to employ them. People have hardly yet waked up to the fact that this refusal, in a highly industrial State, amounts to a very vigorous form of persecution.

If this danger were adequately realized, it would be possible to rouse public opinion, and to secure that a man's beliefs should not be considered in appointing him to a post. The protection of minorities is vitally important; and even the most orthodox of us may find himself in a minority some day, so that we all have an interest in restraining the tyranny of majorities. Nothing except public opinion can solve this problem. Socialism would make it somewhat more acute, since it would eliminate the opportunities that now arise through exceptional employers. Every increase in the size of industrial undertakings makes it worse, since it diminishes the number of independent employers. The battle must be fought exactly as the battle of religious toleration was fought. And as in that case, so in this, a decay in the intensity of belief is likely to prove the decisive factor. While men were convinced of the absolute truth of Catholicism or Protestantism, as the case might be, they were willing to persecute on account of them. While men are quite certain of their modern creeds, they will persecute on their behalf. Some element of doubt is essential to the practice, though not to the theory, of toleration. And this brings me to my other point, which concerns the aims of education.

If there is to be toleration in the world, one of the things taught in schools must be the habit of weighing evidence, and the practice of not giving full assent to propositions which there is no reason to believe true. For example, the art of reading the newspapers should be taught. The schoolmaster should select some incident which happened a good many years ago, and roused political passions in its day. He should then read to the school children what was said by the newspapers on one side, what was said by those on the other, and some impartial account of what really happened. He should show how, from the biased account of either side, a practised reader could infer what really happened, and he should make them understand that everything in newspapers is more or less untrue.

The cynical scepticism which would result from this teaching would make the children in later life immune from those appeals to idealism by which decent people are induced to further the schemes of scoundrels.

History should be taught in the same way. Napoleon's campaigns of 1813 and 1814, for instance, might be studied in the *Moniteur*, leading up to the surprise which Parisians felt when they saw the Allies arriving under the walls of Paris after they had (according to the official bulletins) been beaten by Napoleon in every battle. In the more advanced classes, students should be encouraged to count the number of times that Lenin has been assassinated by Trotsky, in order to learn contempt for death. Finally, they should be given a school history approved by the Government, and asked to infer what a French school history would say about our wars with France. All this would be a far better training in citizenship than the trite moral maxims by which some people believe that civic duty can be inculcated.

It must, I think, be admitted that the evils of the world are due to moral defects quite as much as to lack of intelligence. But the human race has not hitherto discovered any method of eradicating moral defects; preaching and exhortation only add hypocrisy to the previous list of vices. Intelligence, on the contrary, is easily improved by methods known to every competent educator. Therefore, until some method of teaching virtue has been discovered, progress will have to be sought by improvement of intelligence rather than of morals. One of the chief obstacles to intelligence is credulity, and credulity could be enormously diminished by instruction as to the prevalent forms of mendacity. Credulity is a greater evil in the present day than it ever was before, because, owing to the growth of education, it is much easier than it used to be to spread misinformation, and, owing to democracy, the spread of misinformation is more important than in former times to the holders of power. Hence the increase in the circulation of newspapers.

If I am asked how the world is to be induced to adopt these two maxims—namely (1) that jobs should be given to people on account of their fitness to perform them; (2) that one aim of education should be to cure people of the habit of believing propositions for which there is no evidence—I can only say that it must be done by generating an enlightened public opinion. And an enlightened public opinion can only be generated by the efforts of those who desire that it should exist. I do not believe that the economic changes advocated by Socialists will, of themselves, do anything towards curing the evils we have been considering. I think that, whatever happens in politics, the trend of economic development will make the preservation of mental freedom increasingly difficult, unless public opinion insists that the employer shall control nothing in the life of the employee except his work. Freedom in education could easily be secured, if it were desired, by limiting the function of the State to inspection and payment, and confining inspection rigidly to the definite instruction. But that, as things stand, would leave education in the hands of the Churches, because, unfortunately, they are more anxious to teach their beliefs than Freethinkers are to teach their doubts. It would, however, give a free field, and would make it possible for a liberal education to be given if it were really desired. More than that ought not to be asked of the law.

My plea is for the spread of the scientific temper, which is an altogether different thing from the knowledge of scientific results. The scientific temper is capable of regenerating mankind and providing an issue for all our troubles. The results of science, in the form of mechanism, poison gas, and the yellow press, bid fair to lead to the total downfall of our civilization. It is a curious antithesis, which, a Martian might contemplate with amused detachment. But for us it is a matter of life and death. Upon its issue depends the question whether our grandchildren are to live in a happier world, or are to exterminate each other by scientific methods.

ON THE VALUE OF SCEPTICISM

I wish to propose a doctrine which may, I fear, appear wildly paradoxical and subversive. The doctrine in question is this: that it is undesirable to believe a proposition when there is no ground whatever for supposing it true. I must, of course, admit that if such an opinion became common it would completely transform our social life and our political system; since both are at present faultless, this must weigh against it. I am also aware (what is more serious) that it would tend to diminish the incomes of clairvoyants, bookmakers, bishops, and others who live on the irrational hopes of those who have done nothing to deserve good fortune here or hereafter. In spite of these grave arguments, I maintain that a case can be made out of my paradox, and I shall try to set it forth.

First of all, I wish to guard myself against being thought to take up an extreme position. I am a British Whig, with a British love of compromise and moderation. A story is told of Pyrrho, the founder of Pyrrhonism (which was the old name for scepticism). He maintained that we never know enough to be sure that one course of action is wiser than another. In his youth, when he was taking his constitutional one afternoon, he saw his teacher in philosophy (from whom he had imbibed his principles) with his head stuck in a ditch, unable to get out. After contemplating him for some time, he walked on, maintaining that there was no sufficient ground for thinking he would do any good by pulling the man out. Others, less sceptical, effected a rescue, and blamed Pyrrho for his heartlessness. But his teacher, true to his principles, praised him for his consistency. Now I do not advocate such heroic scepticism as that. I am prepared to admit the ordinary beliefs of common sense, in practice if not in theory. I am prepared to admit any well-established result of science, not as certainly true, but as sufficiently probable to afford a basis for rational action. If it is announced that there is to be an eclipse of the moon on such-and-such a date, I think it worth while to look and see whether it is taking place. Pyrrho would have thought otherwise. On this ground, I feel justified in claiming that I advocate a middle position.

There are matters about which those who have investigated them are agreed; the dates of eclipses may serve as an illustration. There are other matters about which experts are not agreed. Even when the experts all agree, they may well be mistaken. Einstein's view as to the magnitude of the deflection of light by gravitation would have been rejected by all experts not many years ago, yet it proved to be right. Nevertheless the opinion of experts, when it is unanimous, must be accepted by non-experts as more likely to be right than the opposite opinion. The scepticism that I advocate amounts only to this: (1) that when the experts are agreed, the opposite opinion cannot be held to be certain; (2) that when they are agreed, no opinion can be regarded as certain by a non-expert; and (3) that when they all hold that no sufficient grounds for a positive opinion exist, the ordinary man would do well to suspend his judgment.

These propositions may seem mild, yet, if accepted, they would absolutely revolutionize human life.

The opinions for which people are willing to fight and persecute all belong to one of the three classes which this scepticism condemns. When there are ra-

tional grounds for an opinion, people are content to
set them forth and wait for them to operate. In such
cases, people do not hold their opinions with passion;
they hold them calmly, and set forth their reasons
quietly. The opinions that are held with passion are
always those for which no good ground exists; indeed
the passion is the measure of the holder's lack of rational conviction. Opinions in politics and religion are
almost always held passionately. Except in China, a
man is thought a poor creature unless he has strong
opinions on such matters; people hate sceptics far more
than they hate the passionate advocates of opinions
hostile to their own. It is thought that the claims of
practical life demand opinions on such questions, and
that, if we became more rational, social existence
would be impossible. I believe the opposite of this,
and will try to make it clear why I have this belief.

Take the question of unemployment in the years
after 1920. One party held that it was due to the
wickedness of trade unions, another that it was due to
the confusion on the Continent. A third party, while
admitting that these causes played a part, attributed
most of the trouble to the policy of the Bank of England in trying to increase the value of the pound ster-
ling. This third party, I am given to understand, con-
tained most of the experts, but no one else. Politicians
do not find any attractions in a view which does not
lend itself to party declamation, and ordinary mortals
prefer views which attribute misfortune to the ma-
chinations of their enemies. Consequently people
fight for and against quite irrelevant measures, while
the few who have a rational opinion are not listened
to because they do not minister to any one's passions.
To produce converts, it would have been necessary to
persuade people that the Bank of England is wicked.
To convert Labour, it would have been necessary to
show that directors of the Bank of England are hostile
to trade unionism; to convert the Bishop of London, it
would have been necessary to show that they are

"immoral." It would be thought to follow that their views on currency are mistaken.

Let us take another illustration. It is often said that socialism is contrary to human nature, and this assertion is denied by socialists with the same heat with which it is made by their opponents. The late Dr. Rivers, whose death cannot be sufficiently deplored, discussed this question in a lecture at University College, published in his posthumous book on *Psychology and Politics*. This is the only discussion of this topic known to me that can lay claim to be scientific. It sets forth certain anthropological data which show that socialism is not contrary to human nature in Melanesia; it then points out that we do not know whether human nature is the same in Melanesia as in Europe; and it concludes that the only way of finding out whether socialism is contrary to European human nature is to try it. It is interesting that on the basis of this conclusion he was willing to become a Labour candidate. But he would certainly not have added to the heat and passion in which political controversies are usually enveloped.

I will now venture on a topic which people find even more difficulty in treating dispassionately, namely marriage customs. The bulk of the population of every country is persuaded that all marriage customs other than its own are immoral, and that those who combat this view do so only in order to justify their own loose lives. In India, the remarriage of widows is traditionally regarded as a thing too horrible to contemplate. In Catholic countries divorce is thought very wicked, but some failure of conjugal fidelity is tolerated, at least in men. In America divorce is easy, but extra-conjugal relations are condemned with the utmost severity. Mohammedans believe in polygamy, which we think degrading. All these differing opinions are held with extreme vehemence, and very cruel persecutions are inflicted upon those who contravene them. Yet no one in any of the various countries makes the slightest attempt to show that the custom of his own country contributes more to human happiness than the custom of others.

When we open any scientific treatise on the subject, such as (for example) Westermarck's *History of Human Marriage*, we find an atmosphere extraordinarily different from that of popular prejudice. We find that every kind of custom has existed, many of them such as we should have supposed repugnant to human nature. We think we can understand polygamy, as a custom forced upon women by male oppressors. But what are we to say of the Tibetan custom, according to which one woman has several husbands? Yet travellers in Tibet assure us that family life there is at least as harmonious as in Europe. A little of such reading must soon reduce any candid person to complete scepticism, since there seem to be no data enabling us to say that one marriage custom is better or worse than another. Almost all involve cruelty and intolerance towards offenders against the local code, but otherwise they have nothing in common. It seems that sin is geographical. From this conclusion, it is only a small step to the further conclusion that the notion of "sin" is illusory, and that the cruelty habitually practised in punishing it is unnecessary. It is just this conclusion which is so unwelcome to many minds, since the infliction of cruelty with a good conscience is a delight to moralists. That is why they invented Hell.

Nationalism is of course an extreme example of fervent belief concerning doubtful matters. I think it may be safely said that any scientific historian, writing now a history of the Great War, is bound to make statements which, if made during the war, would have exposed him to imprisonment in every one of the belligerent countries on both sides. Again, with the exception of China, there is no country where people tolerate the truth about themselves; at ordinary times the truth is only thought ill-mannered, but in war-time it is thought criminal. Opposing systems of violent belief are built up, the falsehood of which is evident from the fact that they are believed only by those who share the same national bias. But the application of reason to these systems of belief is thought as wicked as the application of reason to religious dogmas was formerly thought. When people are challenged as to why scepticism in such matters should be wicked, the only answer is that myths help to win wars, so that a rational nation would be killed rather than kill. The view that there is something shameful in saving one's skin by wholesale slander of foreigners is one which, so far as I know, has hitherto found no supporters among professional moralists outside the ranks of Quakers. If it is suggested that a rational nation would find ways of keeping out of wars altogether, the answer is usually more abuse.

What would be the effect of a spread of rational scepticism? Human events spring from passions, which generate systems of attendant myths. Psychoanalysts have studied the individual manifestations of this process in lunatics, certified and uncertified. A man who has suffered some humiliation invents a theory that he is King of England, and develops all kinds of ingenious explanations of the fact that he is not treated with that respect which his exalted position demands. In this case, his delusion is one with which his neighbours do not sympathize, so they lock him up. But if, instead of asserting only his own greatness, he asserts the greatness of his nation or his class or his creed, he wins hosts of adherents, and becomes a political or religious leader, even if, to the impartial outsider, his views seem just as absurd as those found in asylums. In this way a collective insanity grows up, which follows laws very similar to those of individual insanity. Every one knows that it is dangerous to dispute with a lunatic who thinks he is King of England; but as he is isolated, he can be overpowered. When a whole nation shares a delusion, its anger is of the same kind as that of an individual lunatic if its pretensions are disputed, but nothing short of war can compel it to submit to reason.

The part played by intellectual factors in human behaviour is a matter as to which there is much disagreement among psychologists. There are two quite distinct questions: (1) how far are beliefs operative as causes of actions? (2) how far are beliefs derived from logically adequate evidence, or capable of being so derived? On both questions, psychologists are agreed in giving a much smaller place to the intellectual factors than the plain man would give, but within this general agreement there is room for considerable differences of degree. Let us take the two questions in succession.

(1) How far are beliefs operative as causes of action? Let us not discuss the question theoretically, but let us take an ordinary day of an ordinary man's life. He begins by getting up in the morning, probably from force of habit, without the intervention of any belief. He eats his breakfast, catches his train, reads his newspaper, and goes to his office, all from force of habit. There was a time in the past when he formed these habits, and in the choice of the office, at least, belief played a part. He probably believed, at the time, that the job offered him there was as good as he was likely to get. In most men, belief plays a part in the original choice of a career, and therefore, derivatively, in all that is entailed by this choice.

At the office, if he is an underling, he may continue to act merely from habit, without active volition, and without the explicit intervention of belief. It might be thought that, if he adds up the columns of figures, he believes the arithmetical rules which he employs. But that would be an error; these rules are mere habits of his body, like those of a tennis player. They were acquired in youth, not from an intellectual belief that they corresponded to the truth, but to please the schoolmaster, just as a dog learns to sit on its hind legs and beg for food. I do not say that all education is of this sort, but certainly most learning of the three R's is.

If, however, our friend is a partner or director, he may be called upon during his day to make difficult decisions of policy. In these decisions it is probable that belief will play a part. He believes that some things will go up and others will go down, that so-and-so is a sound man, and such-and-such on the verge of bankruptcy. On these beliefs he acts. It is just because he is called upon to act on beliefs rather than mere habits that he is considered such a much greater man than a mere clerk, and is able to get so much more money— provided his beliefs are true.

In his home-life there will be much the same proportion of occasions when belief is a cause of action. At ordinary times, his behaviour to his wife and children will be governed by habit, or by instinct modified by habit. On great occasions—when he proposes marriage, when he decides what school to send his son to, or when he finds reason to suspect his wife of unfaithfulness—he cannot be guided wholly by habit. In proposing marriage, he may be guided more by instinct, or he may be influenced by the belief that the lady is rich. If he is guided by instinct, he no doubt believes that the lady possesses every virtue, and this may seem to him to be a cause of his action, but in fact it is merely another effect of the instinct which alone suffices to account for his action. In choosing a school for his son, he probably proceeds in much the same way as in making difficult business decisions; here belief usually plays an important part. If evidence comes into his possession showing that his wife has been unfaithful, his behaviour is likely to be purely instinctive, but the instinct is set in operation by a belief, which is the first cause of everything that follows.

Thus, although beliefs are not directly responsible for more than a small part of our actions, the actions for which they are responsible are among the most important, and largely determine the general structure of our lives. In particular, our religious and political actions are associated with beliefs.

(2) I come now to our second question, which is itself twofold: (*a*) how far are beliefs in fact based upon evidence? (*b*) how far is it possible or desirable that they should be?

(*a*) The extent to which beliefs are based upon evidence is very much less than believers suppose. Take the kind of action which is most nearly rational: the investment of money by a rich City man. You will often find that his view (say) on the question whether the French franc will go up or down depends upon his political sympathies, and yet is so strongly held that he is prepared to risk money on it. In bankruptcies it often appears that some sentimental factor was the original cause of ruin. Political opinions are hardly ever based upon evidence, except in the case of civil servants, who are forbidden to give utterance to them. There are of course exceptions. In the tariff reform controversy which began several years ago, most manufacturers supported the side that would increase their own incomes, showing that their opinions were really based on evidence, however little their utterances would have led one to suppose so. We have here a complication. Freudians have accustomed us to "rationalizing," i.e. the process of inventing what seem to ourselves rational grounds for a decision or opinion that is in fact quite irrational. But there is, especially in English-speaking countries, a converse process which may be called "irrationalizing." A shrewd man will sum up, more or less subconsciously, the pros and cons of a question from a selfish point of view. (Unselfish considerations seldom weigh subconsciously except where one's children are concerned.) Having come to a sound egoistic decision by the help of the unconscious, a man proceeds to invent, or adopt from others, a set of high-sounding phrases showing how he is pursuing the public good at immense personal sacrifice. Anybody who believes that these phrases give his real reasons must suppose him quite incapable of judging evidence, since the supposed public good is not going to result from his action. In this case a man appears less rational than he is; what is still more curious, the irrational part of him is conscious and the rational part unconscious. It is this trait in our characters that has made the English and Americans so successful.

Shrewdness, when it is genuine, belongs more to the unconscious than to the conscious part of our nature. It is, I suppose, the main quality required for success in business. From a moral point of view, it is a humble quality, since it is always selfish; yet it suffices to keep men from the worst crimes. If the Germans had had it, they would not have adopted the unlimited submarine campaign. If the French had had it, they would not have behaved as they did in the Ruhr. If Napoleon had had it, he would not have gone to war again after the Treaty of Amiens. It may be laid down as a general rule to which there are few exceptions that, when people are mistaken as to what is to their own interest, the course that they believe to be wise is more harmful to others than the course that really is wise. Therefore anything that makes people better judges of their own interest does good. There are innumerable examples of men making fortunes because, on moral grounds, they did something which they believed to be contrary to their own interests. For instance, among early Quakers there were a number of shopkeepers who adopted the practice of asking no more for their goods than they were willing to accept, instead of bargaining with each customer, as everybody else did. They adopted this practice because they held it to be a lie to ask more than they would take. But the convenience to customers was so great that everybody came to their shops, and they grew rich. (I forget where I read this, but if my memory serves me it was in some reliable source.) The same policy *might* have been adopted from shrewdness, but in fact no one was sufficiently shrewd. Our unconscious is more malevolent than it pays us to be;

therefore the people who do most completely what is in fact to their interest are those who deliberately, on moral grounds, do what they believe to be against their interest. Next to them come the people who try to think out rationally and consciously what is to their own interest, eliminating as far as possible the influence of passion. Third come the people who have instinctive shrewdness. Last of all come the people whose malevolence overbalances their shrewdness, making them pursue the ruin of others in ways that lead to their own ruin. This last class embraces 90 per cent. of the population of Europe.

I may seem to have digressed somewhat from my topic, but it was necessary to disentangle unconscious reason, which is called shrewdness, from the conscious variety. The ordinary methods of education have practically no effect upon the unconscious, so that shrewdness cannot be taught by our present technique. Morality, also, except where it consists of mere habit, seems incapable of being taught by present methods; at any rate I have never noticed any beneficent effect upon those who are exposed to frequent exhortations. Therefore on our present lines any deliberate improvement must be brought about by intellectual means. We do not know how to teach people to be shrewd or virtuous, but we do know, within limits, how to teach them to be rational: it is only necessary to reverse the practice of education authorities in every particular. We may hereafter learn to create virtue by manipulating the ductless glands and stimulating or restraining their secretions. But for the present it is easier to create rationality than virtue—meaning by "rationality" a scientific habit of mind in forecasting the effects of our actions.

(b) This brings me to the question: How far could or should men's actions be rational? Let us take "should" first. There are very definite limits, to my mind, within which rationality should be confined; some of the most important departments of life are ruined by the invasion of reason. Leibniz in his old age told a correspondent that he had only once asked a lady to marry him, and that was when he was fifty. "Fortunately," he added, "the lady asked time to consider. This gave me also time to consider, and I withdrew the offer." Doubtless his conduct was very rational, but I cannot say that I admire it.

Shakespeare puts "the lunatic, the lover, and the poet" together, as being "of imagination all compact." The problem is to keep the lover and the poet, without the lunatic. I will give an illustration. In 1919 I saw *The Trojan Women* acted at the Old Vic. There is an unbearably pathetic scene where Astyanax is put to death by the Greeks for fear he should grow up into a second Hector. There was hardly a dry eye in the theatre, and the audience found the cruelty of the Greeks in the play hardly credible. Yet those very people who wept were, at that very moment, practising that very cruelty on a scale which the imagination of Euripides could have never contemplated. They had lately voted (most of them) for a Government which prolonged the blockade of Germany after the armistice, and imposed the blockade of Russia. It was known that these blockades caused the death of immense numbers of children, but it was felt desirable to diminish the population of enemy countries: the children, like Astyanax, might grow up to emulate their fathers. Euripides the poet awakened the lover in the imagination of the audience; but lover and poet were forgotten at the door of the theatre, and the lunatic (in the shape of the homicidal maniac) controlled the political actions of these men and women who thought themselves kind and virtuous.

Is it possible to preserve the lover and the poet without preserving the lunatic? In each of us, all three exist in varying degrees. Are they so bound up together that when the one is brought under control the others perish? I do not believe it. I believe there is in each of us a certain energy which must find vent in art, in passionate love, or in passionate hate, according to circumstances. Respectability, regularity, and routine—the whole cast-iron discipline of a modern industrial society—have atrophied the artistic impulse, and imprisoned love so that it can no longer be generous and free and creative, but must be either stuffy or furtive. Control has been applied to the very things which should be free, while envy, cruelty, and hate sprawl at large with the blessing of nearly the whole bench of Bishops. Our instinctive apparatus consists of two parts—the one tending to further our own life and that of our descendants, the other tending to thwart the lives of supposed rivals. The first includes the joy of life, and love, and art, which is psychologically an offshoot of love. The second includes competition, patriotism, and war. Conventional morality does everything to suppress the first and encourage the second. True morality would do the exact opposite. Our dealings with those whom we love may be safely left to instinct; it is our dealings with those whom we hate that ought to be brought under the dominion of reason. In the modern world, those whom we effectively hate are distant groups, especially foreign nations. We conceive them abstractly, and deceive ourselves into the belief that acts which are really embodiments of hatred are done from love of justice or some such lofty motive. Only a large measure of scepticism can tear away the veils which hide this truth from us. Having achieved that, we could begin to build a new morality, not based on envy and restriction, but on the wish for a full life and the realization that other human beings are a help and not a hindrance when once the madness of envy has been cured. This is not a Utopian hope; it was partially realized in Elizabethan England. It could be realized tomorrow if men would learn to pursue their own happiness rather than the misery of others. This is no impossibly austere morality, yet its adoption would turn our earth into a paradise.

ON YOUTHFUL CYNICISM

Any person who visits the Universities of the Western world is liable to be struck by the fact that the intelligent young of the present day are cynical to a far greater extent than was the case formerly. This is not true of Russia, India, China, or Japan; I believe it is the case in Czechoslovakia, Jugoslavia, and Poland, nor by any means universally in Germany, but it certainly is a notable characteristic of intelligent youth in England, France, and the United States. To understand why youth is cynical in the West, we must also understand why it is not cynical in the East.

Young men in Russia are not cynical because they accept, on the whole, the Communist philosophy, and they have a great country full of natural resources, ready to be exploited by the help of intelligence. The young have therefore a career before them which they feel to be worth while. You do not have to consider the ends of life when in the course of creating Utopia you are laying a pipe-line, building a railway, or teaching peasants to use Ford tractors simultaneously on a four-mile front. Consequently the Russian youth are vigorous and filled with ardent beliefs.

In India the fundamental belief of the earnest young is in the wickedness of England: from this premise, as from the existence of Descartes, it is possible to deduce a whole philosophy. From the fact that England is Christian, it follows that Hinduism or Mohammedanism, as the case may be, is the only true religion. From the fact that England is capitalistic and industrial, it follows, according to the temperament of the logician concerned, either that everybody ought to spin with a spinning-wheel, or that protective duties ought to be imposed to develop native industrialism and capitalism as the only weapons with which to combat those of the British. From the fact that the British hold India by physical force, it follows that only moral force is admirable. The persecution of nationalist activities in India is just sufficient to make them heroic, and not sufficient to make them seem futile. In this way the Anglo-Indians save the intelligent youth of India from the blight of cynicism.

In China hatred of England has also played its part, but a much smaller part than in India because the English have never conquered the country. The Chinese youth combine patriotism with a genuine enthusiasm for Occidentalism, in the kind of way that was common in Japan fifty years ago. They want the Chinese people to be enlightened, free, and prosperous, and they have their work cut out to produce this result. Their ideals are, on the whole, those of the nineteenth century, which in China have not yet begun to seem antiquated. Cynicism in China was associated with the officials of the Imperial regime and survived among the warring militarists who have distracted the country since 1911, but it has no place in the mentality of the modern intellectuals.

In Japan the outlook of young intellectuals is not unlike that which prevailed on the Continent of Europe between 1815 and 1848. The watchwords of Liberalism are still potent: parliamentary government, liberty of the subject, free thought and free speech. The struggle for these against traditional feudalism and autocracy is quite sufficient to keep young men busy and enthusiastic.

To the sophisticated youth of the West all this ardour seems a trifle crude. He is firmly persuaded that having studied everything impartially, he has seen through everything and found that there is "nothing left remarkable beneath the visiting moon." There are, of course, plenty of reasons for this in the teachings of the old. I do not think these reasons go to the root of the matter, for in other circumstances the young react against the teaching of the old and achieve a gospel of their own. If the Occidental youth of the present day react only by cynicism, there must be some special reason for this circumstance. Not only are the young unable to believe what they are told, but they seem also unable to believe anything else. This is a peculiar state of affairs, which deserves investigation. Let us first take some of the old ideals one by one and see why they no longer inspire the old loyalties. We may enumerate among such ideals: religion, country, progress, beauty, truth. What is wrong with these in the eyes of the young?

Religion.—The trouble here is partly intellectual, partly social. For intellectual reasons few able men have now the same intensity of religious belief as was possible for, say, St. Thomas Aquinas. The God of most moderns is a little vague, and apt to degenerate into a Life Force or a "power not ourselves that makes for righteousness." Even believers are concerned much more with the effects of religion in this world than with that other world that they profess to believe in; they are not nearly so sure that this world was created for the glory of God as they are that God is a useful hypothesis for improving this world. By subordinating God to the needs of this sublunary life, they cast suspicion upon the genuineness of their faith. They seem to think that God, like the Sabbath, was made for man. There are also sociological reasons for not accepting the Churches as the basis of a modern idealism. The Churches, through their endowments, have become bound up with the defence of property. Moreover, they are connected with an oppressive ethic, which condemns many pleasures that to the young appear harmless and inflicts many torments that to the sceptical appear unnecessarily cruel. I have known earnest young men who accepted wholeheartedly the teaching of Christ; they found themselves in opposition to official Christianity, outcasts and victims of persecution, quite as much as if they had been militant Atheists.

Country.—Patriotism has been in many times and places a passionate belief to which the best minds could give full assent. It was so in England in the time of Shakespeare, in Germany in the time of Fichte, in Italy in the time of Mazzini. It is so still in Poland, China, and Outer Mongolia. In the Western nations it is still immensely powerful: it controls politics, public expenditure, military preparations, and so on. But the intelligent youth are unable to accept it as an adequate ideal; they perceive that it is all very well for oppressed nations, but that as soon as an oppressed nation achieves its freedom, the nationalism which was formerly heroic becomes oppressive. The Poles, who had the sympathy of idealists ever since Maria Teresa "wept but took," have used their freedom to organize oppression in Ukrainia. The Irish, upon whom the British had inflicted civilization for eight hundred years, have used their freedom to pass laws preventing the publication of many good books. The spectacle of the Poles murdering Ukrainians and the Irish murdering literature makes nationalism seem a somewhat inadequate idea even for a small nation. But when it comes to a powerful nation, the argument is even stronger. The Treaty of Versailles was not very encouraging to those who had had the luck not to be killed in defending the ideals which their rulers betrayed. Those who during the war averred that they were combating militarism became at its conclusion the leading militarists in their respective countries. Such facts have made it obvious to all intelligent young men that patriotism is the chief curse of our age and will bring civilization to an end if it cannot be mitigated.

Progress.—This is a nineteenth century ideal which has too much Babbitt about it for the sophisticated youth. Measurable progress is necessarily in unimportant things, such as the number of motor-cars made, or the number of peanuts consumed. The really important things are not measurable and are therefore not suitable for the methods of the booster. Moreover, many modern inventions tend to make people silly. I might instance the radio, the talkies, and poison gas. Shakespeare measured the excellence of an age by its style in poetry (see Sonnet XXXII), but his mode of measurement is out of date.

Beauty.—There is something that sounds old-fashioned about beauty, though it is hard to say why. A modern painter would be indignant if he were accused of seeking beauty. Most artists nowadays appear to be inspired by some kind of rage against the world so that they wish rather to give significant pain than to afford serene satisfaction. Moreover many kinds of beauty require that a man should take himself more seriously than is possible for an intelligent modern. A prominent citizen of a small city State, such as Athens or Florence, could without difficulty feel himself important. The earth was the centre of the Universe, man was the purpose of creation, his own city showed man at his best, and he himself was among the best in his own city. In such circumstances Aeschylus or Dante could take his own joys or sorrows seriously. He could feel that the emotions of the individual matter, and that tragic occurrences deserve to be celebrated in immortal verse. But the modern man, when misfortune assails him, is conscious of himself as a unit in a statistical total; the past and the future stretch before him in a dreary procession of trivial defeats. Man himself appears as a somewhat ridiculous strutting animal, shouting and fussing during a brief interlude between infinite silences. "Unaccommodated man is no more but such a poor, bare, forked animal," says King Lear, and the idea drives him to madness because it is unfamiliar. But to the modern man the idea is familiar and drives him only to triviality.

Truth.—In old days truth was absolute, eternal, and superhuman. Myself when young accepted this view and devoted a misspent youth to the search for truth. But a whole host of enemies have arisen to slay truth: pragmatism, behaviorism, psychologism, relativity-physics. Galileo and the Inquisition disagreed as to whether the earth went round the sun or the sun went round the earth. Both agreed in thinking that there was a great difference between these two opinions. The point on which they agreed was the one on which they were both mistaken: the difference is only one of words. In old days it was possible to worship truth; indeed the sincerity of the worship was demonstrated by the practice of human sacrifice. But it is difficult to worship a merely human and relative truth. The law of gravitation, according to Eddington, is only a convenient convention of measurement. It is not truer than other views, any more than the metric system is truer than feet and yards.

Nature and Nature's laws lay hid in night;
God said, "Let Newton be," and measurement was
  facilitated.

This sentiment seems lacking in sublimity. When Spinoza believed anything, he considered that he was enjoying the intellectual love of God. The modern man believes either with Marx that he is swayed by economic motives, or with Freud that some sexual motive underlies his belief in the exponential theorem or in the distribution of fauna in the Red Sea. In neither case can he enjoy Spinoza's exaltation.

So far we have been considering modern cynicism in a rationalistic manner, as something that has intellectual causes. Belief, however, as modern psychologists are never weary of telling us, is seldom determined by rational motives, and the same is true of disbelief,

though sceptics often overlook this fact. The causes of
any widespread scepticism are likely to be sociological
rather than intellectual. The main cause always is comfort without power. The holders of power are not cynical, since they are able to enforce their ideals. Victims
of oppression are not cynical, since they are filled with
hate, and hate, like any other strong passion, brings
with it a train of attendant beliefs. Until the advent of
education, democracy, and mass production, intellectuals had everywhere a considerable influence upon the
march of affairs, which was by no means diminished
if their heads were cut off. The modern intellectual
finds himself in a quite different situation. It is by no
means difficult for him to obtain a fat job and a good
income provided he is willing to sell his services to the
stupid rich either as propagandist or as Court jester.
The effect of mass production and elementary education is that stupidity is more firmly entrenched than at
any other time since the rise of civilization. When the
Czarist Government killed Lenin's brother, it did not
turn Lenin into a cynic, since hatred inspired a lifelong activity in which he was finally successful. But in
the more solid countries of the West there is seldom
such potent cause for hatred, or such opportunity of
spectacular revenge. The work of the intellectuals is
ordered and paid for by Governments or rich men,
whose aims probably seem absurd, if not pernicious, to
the intellectuals concerned. But a dash of cynicism
enables them to adjust their consciences to the situation. There are, it is true, some activities in which
wholly admirable work is desired by the powers that be;
the chief of these is science, and the next is public
architecture in America. But if a man's education has
been literary, as is still too often the case, he finds himself at the age of twenty-two with a considerable skill
that he cannot exercise in any manner that appears important to himself. Men of science are not cynical even
in the West, because they can exercise their best brains
with the full approval of the community; but in this

they are exceptionally fortunate among modern intellectuals.

If this diagnosis is right, modern cynicism cannot be cured merely by preaching, or by putting better ideals before the young than those that their pastors and masters fish out from the rusty armoury of outworn superstitions. The cure will only come when intellectuals can find a career that embodies their creative impulses. I do not see any prescription except the old one advocated by Disraeli: "Educate our masters." But it will have to be a more real education than is commonly given at the present day to either proletarians or plutocrats, and it will have to be an education taking some account of real cultural values and not only of the utilitarian desire to produce so many goods that nobody has time to enjoy them. A man is not allowed to practise medicine unless he knows something of the human body, but a financier is allowed to operate freely without any knowledge at all of the multifarious effects of his activities, with the sole exception of the effect upon his bank account. How pleasant a world would be in which no man was allowed to operate on the Stock Exchange unless he could pass an examination in economics and Greek poetry, and in which politicians were obliged to have a competent knowledge of history and modern novels! Imagine a magnate confronted with the question: "If you were to make a corner in wheat, what effect would this have upon German poetry?" Causation in the modern world is more complex and remote in its ramifications than it ever was before, owing to the increase of larger organizations; but those who control these organizations are ignorant men who do not know the hundredth part of the consequences of their actions. Rabelais published his book anonymously for fear of losing his University post. A modern Rabelais would never write the book, because he would be aware that his anonymity would be penetrated by the perfected methods of publicity. The rulers of the world have always been stupid, but have not in the past been so powerful as they are now. It is therefore more important than it used to be to find some way of securing that they shall be intelligent. Is this problem insoluble? I do not think so, but I should be the last to maintain that it is easy.

IS SCIENCE SUPERSTITIOUS?

Modern life is built on science in two respects. On the one hand, we all depend upon scientific inventions and discoveries for our daily bread and for our comforts and amusements. On the other hand, certain habits of mind, connected with a scientific outlook, have spread gradually during the past three centuries from a few men of genius to large sections of the population. These two operations of science are bound up together when we consider sufficiently long periods, but either might exist without the other for several centuries. Until near the end of the eighteenth century the scientific habit of mind did not greatly affect daily life, since it had not led to the great inventions that revolutionized industrial technique. On the other hand, the manner of life produced by science can be taken over by populations which have only certain practical rudiments of scientific knowledge; such populations can make and utilize machines invented elsewhere, and can even make minor improvements in them. If the collective intelligence of mankind were to degenerate, the kind of technique and daily life which science has produced would nevertheless survive, in all probability, for many generations, but it would not survive for ever, because, if seriously disturbed by a cataclysm, it could not be reconstructed.

The scientific outlook, therefore, is a matter of importance to mankind, either for good or evil. But the

scientific outlook itself is twofold, like the artistic outlook. The creator and the appreciator are different people and require quite different habits of mind. The
scientific creator, like every other, is apt to be inspired
by passions to which he gives an intellectualist expression amounting to an undemonstrated faith, without
which he would probably achieve little. The appreciator does not need this kind of faith; he can see things
in proportion and make necessary reservations, and
may regard the creator as a crude and barbaric person
in comparison with himself. As civilization becomes
more diffused and more traditional, there is a tendency
for the habits of mind of the appreciator to conquer
those who might be creators, with the result that the
civilization in question becomes Byzantine and retrospective. Something of this sort seems to be beginning
to happen in science. The simple faith which upheld
the pioneers is decaying at the centre. Outlying nations, such as the Russians, the Japanese, and the
Young Chinese, still welcome science with seventeenth-
century fervour; so do the bulk of the populations of
Western nations. But the high priests begin to weary
of the worship to which they are officially dedicated.
The pious young Luther reverenced a free-thinking
Pope, who allowed oxen to be sacrificed to Jupiter on
the Capitol to promote his recovery from illness. So in
our day those remote from centres of culture have a
reverence for science which its augurs no longer feel.
The "scientific" materialism of the Bolsheviks, like
early German Protestantism, is an attempt to preserve
the old piety in a form which both friends and foes
believe to be new. But their fiery belief in the verbal
inspiration of Newton has only accelerated the spread
of scientific scepticism among the "bourgeois" scientists of the West. Science, as an activity recognized
and encouraged by the State, has become politically
conservative, except where, as in Tennessee, the State
has remained pre-scientific. The fundamental faith of
most men of science in the present day is not in the

importance of preserving the *status quo*. Consequently
they are very willing to claim for science no more than
its due, and to concede much of the claims of other
conservative forces, such as religion.

They are faced, however, with a great difficulty.
While the men of science are in the main conservative,
science is still the chief agent of rapid change in the
world. The emotions produced by the change in Asia,
in Africa, and among the industrial populations of
Europe are often displeasing to those who have a conservative outlook. Hence arises a hesitation as to the
value of science which has contributed to the scepticism of the High Priests. If it stood alone, it might
be unimportant. But it is reinforced by genuine intellectual difficulties which, if they prove insuperable, are
likely to bring the era of scientific discovery to a close.
I do not mean that this will happen suddenly. Russia
and Asia may continue for another century to entertain
the scientific faith which the West is losing. But sooner
or later, if the logical case against this faith is irrefu-
table, it will convince men who, for whatever reason,
may be momentarily weary; and, once convinced, they
will find it impossible to recapture the old glad con-
fidence. The case against the scientific *credo* deserves,
therefore, to be examined with all care.

When I speak of the scientific *credo*, I am not speaking merely of what is logically implied in the view that,
in the main, science is true; I am speaking of something more enthusiastic and less rational—namely, the
system of beliefs and emotions which lead a man to
become a great scientific discoverer. The question is:
Can such beliefs and emotions survive among men who
have the intellectual powers without which scientific
discovery is impossible?

Two very interesting recent books will help us to
see the nature of the problem. The books I mean are:
Burtt's *Metaphysical Foundations of Modern Science*
(1924) and Whitehead's *Science and the Modern
World* (1926). Each of these criticizes the system of

ideas which the modern world owes to Copernicus, Kepler, Galileo, and Newton—the former almost wholly from an historical standpoint, the latter both historically and logically. Dr. Whitehead's book is the more important, because it is not merely critical, but constructive, and aims at supplying an intellectually satisfying basis for future science, which is to be at the same time emotionally satisfying to the extra-scientific aspirations of mankind. I cannot accept the logical arguments advanced by Dr. Whitehead in favour of what may be called the pleasant parts of this theory: while admitting the need of an intellectual reconstruction of scientific concepts, I incline to the view that the new concepts will be just as disagreeable to our non-intellectual emotions as the old ones, and will therefore be accepted only by those who have a strong emotional bias in favour of science. But let us see what the argument is.

There is, to begin with, the historical aspect. "There can be no living science," says Dr. Whitehead, "unless there is a widespread instinctive conviction in the existence of an *order of things,* and in particular, of an *order of Nature.*" Science could only have been created by men who already had this belief, and therefore the original source of the belief must have been pre-scientific. Other elements also went to make up the complex mentality required for the rise of science. The Greek view of life, he maintains, was predominantly dramatic, and therefore tended to emphasize the end rather than the beginning: this was a drawback from the point of view of science. On the other hand, Greek tragedy contributed the idea of Fate, which facilitated the view that events are rendered necessary by natural laws. "Fate in Greek Tragedy becomes the order of Nature in modern thought." The necessitarian view was reinforced by Roman law. The Roman Government, unlike the Oriental despot, acted (in theory at least) not arbitrarily, but in accordance with rules previously laid down. Similarly, Christianity conceived God as acting in accordance with laws, though they were laws which God Himself had made. All this facilitated the rise of the conception of Natural Law, which is one essential ingredient in scientific mentality.

The non-scientific beliefs which inspired the work of sixteenth- and seventeenth-century pioneers are admirably set forth by Dr. Burtt, with the aid of many little-known original sources. It appears, for example, that Kepler's inspiration was, in part, a sort of Zoroastrian sun worship which he adopted at a critical period of his youth. "It was primarily by such considerations as the deification of the sun and its proper placing at the centre of the universe that Kepler in the years of his adolescent fervour and warm imagination was induced to accept the new system." Throughout the Renaissance there is a certain hostility to Christianity, based primarily upon admiration for Pagan antiquity; it did not dare to express itself openly as a rule, but led, for example, to a revival of astrology, which the Church condemned as involving physical determinism. The revolt against Christianity was associated with superstition quite as much as with science—sometimes, as in Kepler's case, with both in intimate union.

But there is another ingredient, equally essential, but absent in the Middle Ages, and not common in antiquity—namely, an interest in "irreducible and stubborn facts." Curiosity about facts is found before the Renaissance in individuals—for example, the Emperor Frederick II and Roger Bacon; but at the Renaissance it suddenly becomes common among intelligent people. In Montaigne one finds it without the interest in Natural Law; consequently Montaigne was not a man of science. A peculiar blend of general and particular interests is involved in the pursuit of science; the particular is studied in the hope that it may throw light upon the general. In the Middle Ages it was thought that, theoretically, the particular could be deduced from general principles; in the Renaissance these general principles fell into disrepute, and the passion for historical antiquity produced a strong interest in particular occurrences. This interest, operating upon minds trained by Greek, Roman, and scholastic traditions, produced at last the mental atmosphere which made Kepler and Galileo possible. But naturally something of this atmosphere surrounds their work, and has travelled with it down to their present-day successors. "Science has never shaken off its origin in the historical revolt of the later Renaissance. It has remained predominantly an anti-rationalistic movement, based upon a naive faith. What reasoning it has wanted has been borrowed from mathematics, which is a surviving relic of Greek rationalism, following the deductive method. Science repudiates philosophy. In other words, it has never cared to justify its faith or to explain its meaning, and has remained blandly indifferent to its refutation by Hume."

Can science survive when we separate it from the superstitions which nourished its infancy? The indifference of science to philosophy has been due, of course, to its amazing success; it has increased the sense of human power, and has therefore been on the whole agreeable, in spite of its occasional conflicts with theological orthodoxy. But in quite recent times science has been driven by its own problems to take an interest in philosophy. This is especially true of the theory of relativity, with its merging of space and time into the single space-time order of events. But it is true also of the theory of quanta, with its apparent need of discontinuous motion. Also, in another sphere, physiology and bio-chemistry are making inroads on psychology which threaten philosophy in a vital spot; Dr. Watson's Behaviourism is the spear-head of this attack, which, while it involves the opposite of respect for philosophic tradition, nevertheless necessarily rests upon a new philosophy of its own. For such reasons science and philosophy can no longer preserve an armed neutrality, but must be either friends or foes. They cannot be friends unless science can pass the examination which philosophy must set as to its premises. If they cannot be friends, they can only destroy each other; it is no longer possible that either alone can remain master of the field.

Dr. Whitehead offers two things, with a view to the philosophical justification of science. On the one hand, he presents certain new concepts, by means of which the physics of relativity and quanta can be built up in a way which is more satisfying intellectually than any that results from piecemeal amendments to the old conception of solid matter. This part of his work, though not yet developed with the fullness that we may hope to see, lies within science as broadly conceived, and is capable of justification by the usual methods which lead us to prefer one theoretical interpretation of a set of facts to another. It is technically difficult, and I shall say no more about it. From our present point of view, the important aspect of Dr. Whitehead's work is its more philosophical portion. He not only offers us a better science, but a philosophy which is to make that science rational, in a sense in which the traditional science has not been rational since the time of Hume. This philosophy is, in the main, very similar to that of Bergson. The difficulty which I feel here is that, in so far as Dr. Whitehead's new concepts can be embodied in formulæ which can be submitted to the ordinary scientific or logical tests, they do not seem to involve his philosophy; his philosophy, therefore, must be accepted on its intrinsic merits. We must not accept it merely on the ground that, if true, it justifies science, for the question at issue is whether science can be justified. We must examine directly whether it seems to us to be true in fact; and here we find ourselves beset with all the old perplexities.

I will take only one point, but it is a crucial one. Bergson, as every one knows, regards the past as surviving in memory, and also holds that nothing is ever really forgotten; on these points it would seem that Dr.

Whitehead agrees with him. Now this is all very well as a poetic way of speaking, but it cannot (I should have thought) be accepted as a scientifically accurate way of stating the facts. If I recollect some past event —say my arrival in China—it is a mere figure of speech to say that I am arriving in China over again. Certain words or images occur when I recollect, and are related to what I am recollecting, both causally and by a certain similarity, often little more than a similarity of logical structure. The scientific problem of the relation of a recollection to a past event remains intact, even if we choose to say that the recollection consists of a survival of the past event. For, if we say this, we must nevertheless admit that the event has changed in the interval, and we shall be faced with the scientific problem of finding the laws according to which it changes. Whether we call the recollection a new event or the old event greatly changed can make no difference to the scientific problem.

The great scandals in the philosophy of science ever since the time of Hume have been causality and induction. We all believe in both, but Hume made it appear that our belief is a blind faith for which no rational ground can be assigned. Dr. Whitehead believes that his philosophy affords an answer to Hume. So did Kant. I find myself unable to accept either answer. And yet, in common with every one else, I cannot help believing that there must be an answer. This state of affairs is profoundly unsatisfactory, and becomes more so as science becomes more entangled with philosophy. We must hope that an answer will be found; but I am quite unable to believe that it has been found.

Science as it exists at present is partly agreeable, partly disagreeable. It is agreeable through the power which it gives us of manipulating our environment, and to a small but important minority it is agreeable because it affords intellectual satisfactions. It is disagreeable because, however we may seek to disguise the fact, it assumes a determinism which involves, theoretically, the power of predicting human actions; in this respect it seems to lessen human power. Naturally people wish to keep the pleasant aspect of science without the unpleasant aspect; but so far the attempts to do so have broken down. If we emphasize the fact that our belief in causality and induction is irrational, we must infer that we do not know science to be true, and that it may at any moment cease to give us the control over the environment for the sake of which we like it. This alternative, however, is purely theoretical: it is not one which a modern man can adopt in practice. If, on the other hand, we admit the claims of scientific method, we cannot avoid the conclusion that causality and induction are applicable to human volitions as much as to anything else. All that has happened during the twentieth century in physics, physiology, and psychology goes to strengthen this conclusion. The outcome seems to be that, though the rational justification of science is theoretically inadequate, there is no method of securing what is pleasant in science without what is unpleasant. We can do so, of course, by refusing to face the logic of the situation; but, if so, we shall dry up the impulse to scientific discovery at its source, which is the desire to understand the world. It is to be hoped that the future will offer some more satisfactory solution of this tangled problem.

"USELESS" KNOWLEDGE

Francis Bacon, a man who rose to eminence by betraying his friends, asserted, no doubt as one of the ripe lessons of experience, that "knowledge is power." But this is not true of *all* knowledge. Sir Thomas Browne wished to know what song the sirens sang, but if he had ascertained this it would not have enabled him to rise from being a magistrate to being High Sheriff of his county. The sort of knowledge that Bacon had in mind was that which we call scientific. In emphasizing the importance of science, he was belatedly carrying on the tradition of the Arabs and the early Middle Ages, according to which knowledge consisted mainly of astrology, alchemy, and pharmacology, all of which were branches of science. A learned man was one who, having mastered these studies, had acquired magical powers. In the early eleventh century, Pope Silvester II, for no reason except that he read books, was universally believed to be a magician in league with the devil. Prospero, who in Shakespeare's time was a mere phantasy, represented what had been for centuries the generally received conception of a learned man, so far at least as his powers of sorcery were concerned. Bacon believed—rightly, as we now know—that science could provide a more powerful magician's wand than any that had been dreamed of by the necromancers of former ages.

The Renaissance, which was at its height in England

at the time of Bacon, involved a revolt against the
utilitarian conception of knowledge. The Greeks had
acquired a familiarity with Homer, as we do with
music-hall songs, because they enjoyed him, and without feeling that they were engaged in the pursuit of
learning. But the men of the sixteenth century could
not begin to understand him without first absorbing a
very considerable amount of linguistic erudition. They
admired the Greeks, and did not wish to be shut out
from their pleasures; they therefore copied them, both
in reading the classics and in other less avowable ways.
Learning, in the Renaissance, was part of the *joie de
vivre*, just as much as drinking or love-making. And
this was true not only of literature, but also of sterner
studies. Everyone knows the story of Hobbes's first
contact with Euclid: opening the book, by chance, at
the theorem of Pythagoras, he exclaimed, "By God,
this is impossible," and proceeded to read the proofs
backwards until, reaching the axioms, he became convinced. No one can doubt that this was for him a
voluptuous moment, unsullied by the thought of the
utility of geometry in measuring fields.

It is true that the Renaissance found a practical use
for the ancient languages in connection with theology.
One of the earliest results of the new feeling for classical Latin was the discrediting of the forged decretals
and the donation of Constantine. The inaccuracies
which were discovered in the Vulgate and the Septua-
gint made Greek and Hebrew a necessary part of the
controversial equipment of Protestant divines. The
republican maxims of Greece and Rome were invoked
to justify the resistance of Puritans to the Stuarts and
of Jesuits to monarchs who had thrown off allegiance
to the Pope. But all this was an effect, rather than a
cause, of the revival of classical learning, which had
been in full swing in Italy for nearly a century before
Luther. The main motive of the Renaissance was mental
delight, the restoration of a certain richness and freedom in art and speculation which had been lost while

ignorance and superstition kept the mind's eye in blinkers.

The Greeks, it was found, had devoted a part of their attention to matters not purely literary or artistic, such as philosophy, geometry, and astronomy. These studies, therefore, were respectable, but other sciences were more open to question. Medicine, it was true, was dignified by the names of Hippocrates and Galen; but in the intervening period it had become almost confined to Arabs and Jews, and inextricably intertwined with magic. Hence the dubious reputation of such men as Paracelsus. Chemistry was in even worse odour, and hardly became respectable until the eighteenth century.

In this way it was brought about that knowledge of Greek and Latin, with a smattering of geometry and perhaps astronomy, came to be considered the intellectual equipment of a gentleman. The Greeks disdained the practical applications of geometry, and it was only in their decadence that they found a use for astronomy in the guise of astrology. The sixteenth and seventeenth centuries, in the main, studied mathematics with Hellenic disinterestedness, and tended to ignore the sciences which had been degraded by their connection with sorcery. A gradual change towards a wider and more practical conception of knowledge, which was going on throughout the eighteenth century, was suddenly accelerated at the end of that period by the French Revolution and the growth of machinery, of which the former gave a blow to gentlemanly culture while the latter offered new and astonishing scope for the exercise of ungentlemanly skill. Throughout the last hundred and fifty years, men have questioned more and more vigorously the value of "useless" knowledge, and have come increasingly to believe that the only knowledge worth having is that which is applicable to some part of the economic life of the community.

In countries such as France and England, which have a traditional educational system, the utilitarian view of knowledge has only partially prevailed. There are still, for example, professors of Chinese in the universities who read the Chinese classics but are unacquainted with the works of Sun Yat-sen, which created modern China. There are still men who know ancient history in so far as it was related by authors whose style was pure, that is to say up to Alexander in Greece and Nero in Rome, but refuse to know the much more important later history because of the literary inferiority of the historians who related it. Even in France and England, however, the old tradition is dying, and in more up-to-date countries, such as Russia and the United States, it is utterly extinct. In America, for example, educational commissions point out that fifteen hundred words are all that most people employ in business correspondence, and therefore suggest that all others should be avoided in the school curriculum. Basic English, a British invention, goes still further, and reduces the necessary vocabulary to eight hundred words. The conception of speech as something capable of aesthetic value is dying out, and it is coming to be thought that the sole purpose of words is to convey practical information. In Russia the pursuit of practical aims is even more whole-hearted than in America: all that is taught in educational institutions is intended to serve some obvious purpose in education or government. The only escape is afforded by theology: the sacred scriptures must be studied by some in the original German, and a few professors must learn philosophy in order to defend dialectical materialism against the criticisms of bourgeois metaphysicians. But as orthodoxy becomes more firmly established, even this tiny loophole will be closed.

Knowledge, everywhere, is coming to be regarded not as a good in itself, or as a means of creating a broad and humane outlook on life in general, but as merely an ingredient in technical skill. This is part of the greater integration of society which has been brought about by scientific technique and military necessity. There is more economic and political interdependence than there was in former times, and therefore there is more social pressure to compel a man to live in a way that his neighbours think useful. Educational establishments, except those for the very rich, or (in England) such as have become invulnerable through antiquity, are not allowed to spend their money as they like, but must satisfy the State that they are serving a useful purpose by imparting skill and instilling loyalty. This is part and parcel of the same movement which has led to compulsory military service, boy scouts, the organization of political parties, and the dissemination of political passion by the Press. We are all more aware of our fellow-citizens than we used to be, more anxious, if we are virtuous, to do them good, and in any case to make them do us good. We do not like to think of anyone lazily enjoying life, however refined may be the quality of his enjoyment. We feel that everybody ought to be doing something to help on the great cause (whatever it may be), the more so as so many bad men are working against it and ought to be stopped. We have not leisure of mind, therefore, to acquire any knowledge except such as will help us in the fight for whatever it may happen to be that we think important.

There is much to be said for the narrowly utilitarian view of education. There is not time to learn everything before beginning to make a living, and undoubtedly "useful" knowledge is *very* useful. It has made the modern world. Without it, we should not have machines or motorcars or railways or aeroplanes; it should be added that we should not have modern advertising or modern propaganda. Modern knowledge has brought about an immense improvement in average health, and at the same time has discovered how to exterminate large cities by poison gas. Whatever is distinctive of our world, as compared with former times, has its source in "useful" knowledge. No community as yet has enough of it, and undoubtedly education must continue to promote it.

It must also be admitted that a great deal of the traditional cultural education was foolish. Boys spent many years acquiring Latin and Greek grammar, without being, at the end, either capable or desirous (except in a small percentage of cases) of reading a Greek or Latin author. Modern languages and history are preferable, from every point of view, to Latin and Greek. They are not only more useful, but they give much more culture in much less time. For an Italian of the fifteenth century, since practically everything worth reading, if not in his own language, was in Greek or Latin, these languages were the indispensable keys to culture. But since that time great literatures have grown up in various modern languages, and the development of civilization has been so rapid that knowledge of antiquity has become much less useful in understanding our problems than knowledge of modern nations and their comparatively recent history. The traditional schoolmasters's point of view, which was admirable at the time of the revival of learning, became gradually unduly narrow, since it ignored what the world has done since the fifteenth century. And not only history and modern languages, but science also, when properly taught, contributes to culture. It is therefore possible to maintain that education should have other aims than direct utility, without defending the traditional curriculum. Utility and culture, when both are conceived broadly, are found to be less incompatible than they appear to the fanatical advocates of either.

Apart, however, from the cases in which culture and direct utility can be combined, there is indirect utility, of various different kinds, in the possession of knowledge which does not contribute to technical efficiency. I think some of the worst features of the modern world could be improved by a greater encouragement of such

knowledge and a less ruthless pursuit of mere professional competence.

When conscious activity is wholly concentrated on
some one definite purpose, the ultimate result, for most
people, is lack of balance accompanied by some form
of nervous disorder. The men who directed German
policy during the war of 1914-18 made mistakes, for
example, as regards the submarine campaign which
brought America on to the side of the Allies, which
any person coming fresh to the subject could have seen
to be unwise, but which they could not judge sanely
owing to mental concentration and lack of holidays.
The same sort of thing may be seen wherever bodies
of men attempt tasks which put a prolonged strain
upon spontaneous impulses. Japanese imperialists, Russian Communists, and German Nazis all had or have
a kind of tense fanaticism which comes of living too
exclusively in the mental world of certain tasks to be
accomplished. When the tasks are as important and
as feasible as the fanatics suppose, the result may be
magnificent; but in most cases narrowness of outlook
has caused oblivion of some powerful counteracting
force, or has made all such forces seem the work of the
devil, to be met by punishment and terror. Men as well
as children have need of play, that is to say, of periods
of activity having no purpose beyond present enjoyment. But if play is to serve its purpose, it must be
possible to find pleasure and interest in matters not
connected with work.

The amusements of modern urban populations tend
more and more to be passive and collective, and to
consist of inactive observation of the skilled activities
of others. Undoubtedly such amusements are much better than none, but they are not as good as would
be those of a population which had, through education, a wider range of intelligent interests not connected with work. Better economic organization, allowing mankind to benefit by the productivity of machines, should lead to a very great increase of leisure,

and much leisure is apt to be tedious except to those who have considerable intelligent activities and interests. If a leisured population is to be happy, it must be an educated population, and must be educated with a view to mental enjoyment as well as to the direct usefulness of technical knowledge.

The cultural element in the acquisition of knowledge, when it is successfully assimilated, forms the character of a man's thoughts and desires, making them concern themselves, in part at least, with large impersonal objects, not only with matters of immediate importance to himself. It has been too readily assumed that, when a man has acquired certain capacities by means of knowledge, he will use them in ways that are socially beneficial. The narrowly utilitarian conception of education ignores the necessity of training a man's purposes as well as his skill. There is in untrained human nature a very considerable element of cruelty, which shows itself in many ways, great and small. Boys at school tend to be unkind to a new boy, or to one whose clothes are not quite conventional. Many women (and not a few men) inflict as much pain as they can by means of malicious gossip. The Spaniards enjoy bull-fights; the British enjoy hunting and shooting. The same cruel impulses take more serious forms in the hunters of Jews in Germany and kulaks in Russia. All imperialism affords scope for them, and in war they become sanctified as the highest form of public duty.

Now while it must be admitted that highly educated people are sometimes cruel, I think there can be no doubt that they are less often so than people whose minds have lain fallow. The bully in a school is seldom a boy whose proficiency in learning is up to the average. When a lynching takes place, the ringleaders are almost invariably very ignorant men. This is not because mental cultivation produces positive humanitarian feelings, though it may do so; it is rather because it gives other interests than the ill-treatment of neighbours, and other sources of self-respect than the assertion of domination. The two things most universally desired are power and admiration. Ignorant men can, as a rule, only achieve either by brutal means, involving the acquisition of physical mastery. Culture gives a man less harmful forms of power and more deserving ways of making himself admired. Galileo did more than any monarch has done to change the world, and his power immeasurably exceeded that of his persecutors. He had therefore no need to aim at becoming a persecutor in his turn.

Perhaps the most important advantage of "useless" knowledge is that it promotes a contemplative habit of mind. There is in the world much too much readiness, not only for action without adequate previous reflection, but also for some sort of action on occasions on which wisdom would consel inaction. People show their bias on this matter in various curious ways. Mephistopheles tells the young student that theory is grey but the tree of life is green, and everyone quotes this as if it were Goethe's opinion, instead of what he supposes the devil would be likely to say to an undergraduate. Hamlet is held up as an awful warning against thought without action, but no one holds up Othello as a warning against action without thought. Professors such as Bergson, from a kind of snobbery towards the practical man, decry philosophy, and say that life at its best should resemble a cavalry charge. For my part, I think action is best when it emerges from a profound apprehension of the universe and human destiny, not from some wildly passionate impulse of romantic but disproportioned self-assertion. A habit of finding pleasure in thought rather than in action is a safeguard against unwisdom and excessive love of power, a means of preserving serenity in misfortune and peace of mind among worries. A life confined to what is personal is likely, sooner or later, to become unbearably painful; it is only by windows into a larger and less fretful cosmos that the more tragic parts of life become endurable.

A contemplative habit of mind has advantages ranging from the most trivial to the most profound. To begin with minor vexations, such as fleas, missing trains, or cantankerous business associates. Such troubles seem hardly worthy to be met by reflections on the excellence of heroism or the transitoriness of all human ills, and yet the irritation to which they give rise destroys many people's good temper and enjoyment of life. On such occasions, there is much consolation to be found in out-of-the-way bits of knowledge which have some real or fancied connection with the trouble of the moment; or even if they have none, they serve to obliterate the present from one's thoughts. When assailed by people who are white with fury, it is pleasant to remember the chapter in Descartes's *Treatise on the Passions* entitled "Why those who grow pale with rage are more to be feared than those who grow red." When one feels impatient over the difficulty of securing international co-operation, one's impatience is diminished if one happens to think of the sainted King Louis IX, before embarking on his crusade, allying himself with the Old Man of the Mountain, who appears in the Arabian Nights as the dark source of half the wickedness in the world. When the rapacity of capitalists grows oppressive, one may be suddenly consoled by the recollection that Brutus, that exemplar of republican virtue, lent money to a city at 40 per cent., and hired a private army to beseige it when it failed to pay the interest.

Curious learning not only makes unpleasant things less unpleasant, but also makes pleasant things more pleasant. I have enjoyed peaches and apricots more since I have known that they were first cultivated in China in the early days of the Han dynasty; that Chinese hostages held by the great King Kaniska introduced them into India, whence they spread to

Persia, reaching the Roman Empire in the first century of our era; that the word "apricot" is derived from the same Latin source as the word "precocious," because the apricot ripens early; and that the A at the beginning was added by mistake, owing to a false etymology. All this makes the fruit taste much sweeter.

About a hundred years ago, a number of well-meaning philanthropists started societies "for the diffusion of useful knowledge," with the results that people have ceased to appreciate the delicious savour of "useless" knowledge. Opening Burton's *Anatomy of Melancholy* at haphazard on a day when I was threatened by that mood, I learnt that there is a "melancholy matter," but that, while some think it may be engendered of all four humours, "Galen holds that it may be engendered of three alone, excluding phlegm or pituita, whose true assertion Valerius and Menardus stiffly maintain, and so doth Fuscius, Montaltus, Montanus. How (say they) can white become black?" In spite of this unanswerable argument, Hercules de Saxonia and Cardan, Guianerius and Laurentius, are (so Burton tells us) of the opposite opinion. Soothed by these historical reflections, my melancholy, whether due to three humours or to four, was dissipated. As a cure for too much zeal, I can imagine few measures more effective than a course of such ancient controversies.

But while the trivial pleasures of culture have their place as a relief from the trivial worries of practical life, the more important merits of contemplation are in relation to the greater evils of life, death and pain and cruelty, and the blind march of nations into unnecessary disaster. For those to whom dogmatic religion can no longer bring comfort, there is need of some substitute, if life is not to become dusty and harsh and filled with trivial self-assertion. The world at present is full of angry self-centred groups, each incapable of viewing human life as a whole, each willing to destroy civilization rather than yield an inch. To this narrowness no amount of technical instruction will provide an antidote. The antidote, in so far as it is matter of individual psychology, is to be found in history, biology, astronomy, and all those studies which, without destroying self-respect, enable the individual to see himself in his proper perspective. What is needed is not this or that specific piece of information, but such knowledge as inspires a conception of the ends of human life as a whole: art and history, acquaintance with the lives of heroic individuals, and some understanding of the strangely accidental and ephemeral position of man in the cosmos—all this touched with an emotion of pride in what is distinctively human, the power to see and to know, to feel magnanimously and to think with understanding. It is from large perceptions combined with impersonal emotion that wisdom most readily springs.

Life, at all times full of pain, is more painful in our time than in the two centuries that preceded it. The attempt to escape from pain drives men to triviality, to self-deception, to the invention of vast collective myths. But these momentary alleviations do but increase the sources of suffering in the long run. Both private and public misfortune can only be mastered by a process in which will and intelligence interact: the part of will is to refuse to shirk the evil or accept an unreal solution, while the part of intelligence is to understand it, to find a cure if it is curable, and, if not, to make it bearable by seeing it in its relations, accepting it as unavoidable, and remembering what lies outside it in other regions, other ages, and the abysses of interstellar space.

WHAT IS THE SOUL?

One of the most painful circumstances of recent advances in science is that each one of them makes us know less than we thought we did. When I was young we all knew, or thought we knew, that a man consists of a soul and a body; that the body is in time and space, but the soul is in time only. Whether the soul survives death was a matter as to which opinions might differ, but that there is a soul was thought to be indubitable. As for the body, the plain man of course considered its existence self-evident, and so did the man of science, but the philosopher was apt to analyze it away after one fashion or another, reducing it usually to ideas in the mind of the man who had the body and anybody else who happened to notice him. The philosopher, however, was not taken seriously, and science remained comfortably materialistic, even in the hands of quite orthodox scientists.

Nowadays these fine old simplicities are lost: physicists assure us that there is no such thing as matter, and psychologists assure us that there is no such thing as mind. This is an unprecedented occurrence. Who ever heard of a cobbler saying that there was no such thing as boots, or a tailor maintaining that all men are really naked? Yet that would have been no odder than what physicists and certain psychologists have been doing. To begin with the latter, some of them attempt to reduce everything that seems to be mental activity to an activity of the body. There are, however, various difficulties in the way of reducing mental activity to physical activity. I do not think we can yet say with any assurance whether these difficulties are or are not insuperable. What we can say, on the basis of physics itself, is that what we have hitherto called our body is really an elaborate scientific construction not corresponding to any physical reality. The modern would-be materialist thus finds himself in a curious position, for, while he may with a certain degree of success reduce the activities of the mind to those of the body, he cannot explain away the fact that the body itself is merely a convenient concept invented by the mind. We find ourselves thus going round and round in a circle: mind is an emanation of body, and body is an invention of mind. Evidently this cannot be quite right, and we have to look for something that is neither mind nor body, out of which both can spring.

Let us begin with the body. The plain man thinks that material objects must certainly exist, since they are evident to the senses. Whatever else may be doubted, it is certain that anything you can bump into must be real; this is the plain man's metaphysic. This is all very well, but the physicist comes along and shows that you never bump into anything: even when you run your head against a stone wall, you do not really touch it. When you think you touch a thing, there are certain electrons and protons, forming part of your body, which are attracted and repelled by certain electrons and protons in the thing you think you are touching, but there is no actual contact. The electrons and protons in your body, becoming agitated by nearness to the other electrons and protons, are disturbed, and transmit a disturbance along your nerves to the brain; the effect in the brain is what is necessary to your sensation of contact, and by suitable experiments this sensation can be made quite deceptive. The electrons and protons themselves, however, are only a crude first approximation, a way of collecting into a bundle either trains of waves or the statistical probabilities of various different kinds of events. Thus matter has become altogether too ghostly to be used as an adequate stick with which to beat the mind. Matter in motion, which used to seem so unquestionable, turns out to be a concept quite inadequate for the needs of physics.

Nevertheless modern science gives no indication whatever of the existence of the soul or mind as an entity; indeed the reasons for disbelieving in it are of very much the same kind as the reasons for disbelieving in matter. Mind and matter were something like the lion and the unicorn fighting for the crown; the end of the battle is not the victory of one or the other, but the discovery that both are only heraldic inventions. The world consists of events, not of things that endure for a long time and have changing properties. Events can be collected into groups by their causal relations. If the causal relations are of one sort, the resulting group of events may be called a physical object, and if the causal relations are of another sort, the resulting group may be called a mind. Any event that occurs inside a man's head will belong to groups of both kinds; considered as belonging to a group of one kind, it is a constituent of his brain, and considered as belonging to a group of the other kind, it is a constituent of his mind.

Thus both mind and matter are merely convenient ways of organizing events. There can be no reason for supposing that either a piece of mind of a piece of matter is immortal. The sun is supposed to be losing matter at the rate of millions of tons a minute. The most essential characteristic of mind is memory, and there is no reason whatever to suppose that the memory associated with a given person survives that person's death. Indeed there is every reason to think the opposite, for memory is clearly connected with a certain kind of brain structure, and since this structure decays at death, there is every reason to suppose that memory also must cease. Although metaphysical materialism cannot be considered true, yet emotionally the world is pretty much the same as it would be if the materialists were in the right. I think the opponents of materialism have always been actuated by two main desires: the first to prove that the mind is immortal, and the second to prove that the ultimate power in the universe is mental rather than physical. In both these respects, I think the materialists were in the right. Our desires, it is true, have considerable power on the earth's surface; the greater part of the land on this planet has a quite different aspect from that which it would have if men had not utilized it to extract food and wealth. But our power is very strictly limited. We cannot at present do anything whatever to the sun or moon or even to the interior of the earth, and there is not the faintest reason to suppose that what happens in regions to which our power does not extend has any mental causes. That is to say, to put the matter in a nutshell, there is no reason to think that except on the earth's surface anything happens because somebody wishes it to happen. And since our power on the earth's surface is entirely dependent upon the supply of energy which the earth derives from the sun, we are necessarily dependent upon the sun, and could hardly realize any of our wishes if the sun grew cold. It is of course rash to dogmatize as to what science may achieve in the future. We may learn to prolong human existence longer than now seems possible, but if there is any truth in modern physics, more particularly in the second law of thermo-dynamics, we cannot hope that the human race will continue for ever. Some people may find this conclusion gloomy, but if we are honest with ourselves, we shall have to admit that what is going to happen many millions of years hence has no very great emotional interest for us here and now. And science, while it diminishes our cosmic pretensions, enormously increases our terrestrial comfort. That is why, in spite of the horror of the theologians, science has on the whole been tolerated.

THE ANCESTRY OF FASCISM

When we compare our age with that of (say) George I, we are conscious of a profound change of intellectual temper, which has been followed by a corresponding change of the tone of politics. In a certain sense, the outlook of two hundred years ago may be called "rational," and that which is most characteristic of our time may be called "antirational." But I want to use these words without implying a complete acceptance of the one temper or a complete rejection of the other. Moreover, it is important to remember that political events very frequently take their colour from the speculations of an earlier time: there is usually a considerable interval between the promulgation of a theory and its practical efficacy. English politics in 1860 were dominated by the ideas expressed by Adam Smith in 1766; German politics to-day are a realization of theories set forth by Fichte in 1807; Russian politics since 1917 have embodied the doctrines of the Communist Manifesto, which dates from 1848. To understand the present age, therefore, it is necessary to go back to a considerably earlier time.

A widespread political doctrine has, as a rule, two very different kinds of causes. On the one hand, there are intellectual antecedents: men who have advanced theories which have grown, by development or reaction, from previous theories. On the other hand, there are economic and political circumstances which predispose people to accept views that minister to certain moods. These alone do not give a complete explanation when, as too often happens, intellectual antecedents are neglected. In the particular case that concerns us, various sections of the post-war world have had certain grounds of discontent which have made them sympathetic to a certain general philosophy invented at a much earlier date. I propose first to consider this philosophy, and then to touch on the reasons for its present popularity.

The revolt against *reason* began as a revolt against *reasoning*. In the first half of the eighteenth century, while Newton ruled men's minds, there was a widespread belief that the road to knowledge consisted in the discovery of simple general laws, from which conclusions could be drawn by deductive ratiocination. Many people forgot that Newton's law of gravitation was based upon a century of careful observation, and imagined that general laws could be discovered by the light of nature. There was natural religion, natural law, natural morality, and so on. These subjects were supposed to consist of demonstrative inferences from self-evident axioms, after the style of Euclid. The political outcome of this point of view was the doctrine of the Rights of Man, as preached during the American and French Revolutions.

But at the very moment when the Temple of Reason seemed to be nearing completion, a mine was laid by which, in the end, the whole edifice was blown sky-high. The man who laid the mine was David Hume. His *Treatise of Human Nature*, published in 1739, has as its subtitle "An attempt to introduce the experimental method of reasoning into moral subjects." This represents the whole of his intention, but only half of his performance. His intention was to substitute observation and induction for deduction from nominally self-evident axioms. In his temper of mind he was a complete Rationalist, though of the Baconian rather than the Aristotelian variety. But his almost unexampled combination of acuteness with intellectual honesty led him to certain devastating conclusions: that induction is a habit without logical justification, and that the belief in causation is little better than a superstition. It followed that science, along with theology, should be relegated to the limbo of delusive hopes and irrational convictions.

In Hume, Rationalism and scepticism existed peacefully side by side. Scepticism was for the study only, and was to be forgotten in the business of practical life. Moreover, practical life was to be governed, as far as possible, by those very methods of science which his scepticism impugned. Such a compromise was only possible for a man who was in equal parts a philosopher and a man of the world; there is also a flavour of aristocratic Toryism in the reservation of an esoteric unbelief for the initiated. The world at large refused to accept Hume's doctrines in their entirety. His followers rejected his scepticism, while his German opponents emphasized it as the inevitable outcome of a merely scientific and rational outlook. Thus as the result of his teaching British philosophy became superficial, while German philosophy became anti-rational —in each case from fear of an unbearable Agnosticism. European thought has never recovered its previous whole-heartedness; among all the successors of Hume, sanity has meant superficiality, and profundity has meant some degree of madness. In the most recent discussions of the philosophy appropriate to quantum physics, the old debates raised by Hume are still proceeding.

The philosophy which has been distinctive of Germany begins with Kant, and begins as a reaction against Hume. Kant was determined to believe in causality, God, immortality, the moral law, and so on, but perceived that Hume's philosophy made all this difficult. He therefore invented a distinction between "pure" reason and "practical" reason. "Pure" reason was concerned with what could be proved, which was not much; "practical" reason was concerned with what was necessary for virtue, which was a great deal. It is, of course, obvious that "pure" reason was simply reason, while "practical" reason was prejudice. Thus Kant brought back into philosophy the appeal to something recognized as outside the sphere of theoretical rationality, which had been banished from the schools ever since the rise of scholasticism.

More important even than Kant, from our point of view, was his immediate successor Fichte, who, passing over from philosophy to politics, inaugurated the movement which has developed into National Socialism. But before speaking of him there is more to be said about the conception of "reason."

In view of the failure to find an answer to Hume, "reason" can no longer be regarded as something absolute, any departure from which is to be condemned on theoretical grounds. Nevertheless, there is obviously a difference, and an important one, between the frame of mind of (say) the philosophical radicals and such people as the early Mohammedan fanatics. If we call the former temper of mind reasonable and the latter unreasonable, it is clear that there has been a growth of unreason in recent times.

I think that what we mean in practice by reason can be defined by three characteristics. In the first place, it relies upon persuasion rather than force; in the second place, it seeks to persuade by means of arguments which the man who uses them believes to be completely valid; and in the third place, in forming opinions, it uses observation and induction as much as possible and intuition as little as possible. The first of these rules out the Inquisition; the second rules out such methods as those of British war propaganda, which Hitler praises on the ground that propaganda "must sink its mental elevation deeper in proportion to the numbers of the mass whom it has to grip"; the third forbids the use of such a major premise as that of President Andrew Jackson *a propos* of the Mississippi, "the God of the Universe intended this great valley to belong to one nation," which was self-evident to him and his hearers, but not easily demonstrated to one who questioned it.

Reliance upon reason, as thus defined, assumes a certain community of interest and outlook between oneself and one's audience. It is true that Mrs. Bond tried it on her ducks, when she cried "come and be killed, for you must be stuffed and my customers filled"; but in general the appeal to reason is thought ineffective with those whom we mean to devour. Those who believe in eating meat do not attempt to find arguments which would seem valid to a sheep, and Nietzsche does not attempt to persuade the mass of the population, whom he calls "the bungled and blotched." Nor does Marx try to enlist the support of capitalists. As these instances show, the appeal to reason is easier when power is unquestioningly confined to an oligarchy. In eighteenth-century England, only the opinions of aristocrats and their friends were important, and these could always be presented in a rational form to other aristocrats. As the political constituency grows larger and more heterogeneous, the appeal to reason becomes more difficult, since there are fewer universally conceded assumptions from which agreement can start. When such assumptions cannot be found, men are driven to rely upon their own intuitions; and since the intuitions of different groups differ, reliance upon them leads to strife and power politics.

Revolts against reason, in this sense, are a recurrent phenomenon in history. Early Buddhism was reasonable; its later forms, and the Hinduism which replaced it in India, were not. In ancient Greece, the Orphics were in revolt against Homeric rationality. From Socrates to Marcus Aurelius, the prominent men in the ancient world were, in the main, rational; after Marcus Aurelius, even the conservative Neo-Platonists were filled with superstition. Except in the Mohammedan world, the claims of reason remained in abeyance until the eleventh century; after that, through scholasticism, the Renaissance, and science, they became increasingly dominant. A reaction set in with Rousseau and Wesley, but was held in check by the triumphs of science and machinery in the nineteenth century. The belief in reason reached its maximum in the 'sixties; since then, it has gradually diminished, and it is still diminishing. Rationalism and anti-rationalism have existed side by side since the beginning of Greek civilization, and each, when it has seemed likely to become completely dominant, has always led, by reaction, to a new outburst of its opposite.

The modern revolt against reason differs in an important respect from most of its predecessors. From the Orphics onwards, the usual aim in the past was salvation—a complex concept involving both goodness and happiness, and achieved, as a rule, by some difficult renunciation. The irrationalists of our time aim, not at salvation, but at power. They thus develop an ethic which is opposed to that of Christianity and of Buddhism; and through their lust of dominion they are of necessity involved in politics. Their genealogy among writers is Fichte, Carlyle, Mazzini, Nietzsche— with supporters such as Treitschke, Rudyard Kipling, Houston Chamberlain, and Bergson. As opposed to this movement, Benthamites and Socialists may be viewed as two wings of one party: both are cosmopolitan, both are democratic, both appeal to economic self-interest. Their differences *inter se* are as to means, not ends, whereas the new movement, which culminates (as yet) in Hitler, differs from both as to ends, and differs even from the whole tradition of Christian civilization.

The end which statesmen should pursue, as conceived by almost all the irrationalists out of whom Fascism has grown, is most clearly stated by Nietzsche. In conscious opposition to Christianity as well as to the utilitarians, he rejects Bentham's doctrines as regards both happiness and the "greatest number." "Man-

kind," he says, "is much more of a means than an end
. . . mankind is merely the experimental material."
The end he proposes is the greatness of exceptional
individuals: "The object is to attain that enormous
energy of greatness which can model the man of the
future by means of discipline and also by means of the
annihilation of millions of the bungled and botched,
and which can yet avoid *going to ruin* at the sight of
the suffering *created thereby*, the like of which has
never been seen before." This conception of the end,
it should be observed, cannot be regarded as itself contrary to reason, since questions of ends are not amen-
able to rational argument. We may *dislike* it—I do
myself—but we cannot *disprove* it any more than
Nietzsche can prove it. There is, none the less, a natural connection with irrationality, since reason demands impartiality, whereas the cult of the great man
always has as its minor premise the assertion: "I am
a great man."

The founders of the school of thought out of which
Fascism has grown all have certain common characteristics. They seek the good in *will* rather than in feeling
or cognition; they value power more than happiness;
they prefer force to argument, war to peace, aristocracy
to democracy, propaganda to scientific impartiality.
They advocate a Spartan form of austerity, as opposed
to the Christian form; that is to say, they view austerity
as a means of obtaining mastery over others, not as a
self-discipline which helps to produce virtue, and happiness only in the next world. The later ones among
them are imbued with popular Darwinism, and regard
the struggle of existence as the source of a higher
species; but it is to be rather a struggle between races
than one between individuals, such as the apostles of
free competition advocated. Pleasure and knowledge,
conceived as ends, appear to them unduly passive. For
pleasure they substitute glory, and, for knowledge, the
pragmatic assertion that what they desire is true. In
Fichte, Carlyle, and Mazzini, these doctrines are still

enveloped in a mantle of conventional moralistic cant; in Nietzsche they first step forth naked and unashamed.

Fichte has received less than his due share of credit for inaugurating this great movement. He began as an abstract metaphysician, but showed even then a certain arbitrary and self-centred disposition. His whole philosophy develops out of the proposition "I am I," as to which he says:—

"The Ego *posits itself* and it *is* in consequence of this bare positing by itself; it is both the agent and the result of the action, the active and that which is produced by the activity; I *am* expresses a deed (*That-handlung*). The Ego is, because it has posited itself."

The Ego, according to this theory, exists because it wills to exist. Presently it appears that the non-Ego also exists because the Ego so wills it; but a non-Ego so generated never becomes really external to the Ego which chooses to posit it. Louis XIV said, "l'état, c'est moi"; Fichte said, "The universe is myself." As Heine remarked in comparing Kant and Robespierre, "in comparison with us Germans, you French are tame and moderate."

Fichte, it is true, explains after a while, that when he says "I" he means "God"; but the reader is not wholly reassured. When, as a result of the Battle of Jena, Fichte had to fly from Berlin, he began to think that he had been too vigorously positing the non-Ego in the shape of Napoleon. On his return in 1807, he delivered his famous "Addresses to the German Nation," in which, for the first time, the complete creed of nationalism was set out. These Addresses begin by explaining that the German is superior to all other moderns, because he alone has a pure language. (The Russians, Turks, and Chinese, not to mention the Eskimos and the Hottentots, also have pure languages, but they were not mentioned in Fichte's history books.) The purity of the German language makes the German alone capable of profundity; he concludes that "to have character and to be German undoubtedly mean the same." But if the German character is to be preserved from foreign corrupting influences, and if the German nation is to be capable of acting as a whole, there must be a new kind of education, which will "mould the Germans into a corporate body." The new education, he says, "must consist essentially in this, that it completely destroys freedom of the will." He adds that will "is the very root of man."

There is to be no external commerce, beyond what is absolutely unavoidable. There is to be universal military service: everybody is to be compelled to fight, not for material well-being, not for freedom, not in defence of the constitution, but under the impulsion of "the devouring flame of higher patriotism, which embraces the nation as the vesture of the eternal, for which the noble-minded man joyfully sacrifices himself, and the ignoble man, who only exists for the sake of the other, must likewise sacrifice himself."

This doctrine, that the "noble" man is the purpose of humanity, and that the "ignoble" man has no claims on his own account, is of the essence of the modern attack on democracy. Christianity taught that every human being has an immortal soul, and that, in this respect, all men are equal; the "rights of man" was only a development of Christian doctrine. Utilitarianism, while it conceded no absolute "rights" to the individual, gave the same weight to one man's happiness as to another's; thus it led to democracy just as much as did the doctrine of natural rights. But Fichte, like a sort of political Calvin, picked out certain men as the elect, and rejected all the rest as of no account.

The difficulty, of course, is to know who are the elect. In a world in which Fichte's doctrine was universally accepted, every man would think that he was "noble," and would join some party of people sufficiently similar to himself to seem to share some of his nobility. These people might be his nation, as in Fichte's case, or his class, as in that of a proletarian communist, or his family, as with Napoleon. There is no objective criterion of "nobility" except success in war; therefore war is the necessary outcome of this creed.

Carlyle's outlook on life was, in the main, derived from Fichte, who was the strongest single influence on his opinions. But Carlyle added something which has been characteristic of the school ever since: a kind of Socialism and solicitude for the proletariat which is really dislike of industrialism and of the *nouveau riche*. Carlyle did this so well that he deceived even Engels, whose book on the English working class in 1844 mentions him with the highest praise. In view of this, we can scarcely wonder that many people were taken in by the socialistic facade in National Socialism.

Carlyle, in fact, still has his dupes. His "hero worship" sounds very exalted; we need, he says, not elected Parliaments, but "Hero-kings, and a whole world not unheroic." To understand this, one must study its translation into fact. Carlyle, in *Past and Present*, holds up the twelfth-century Abbot Samson as a model; but whoever does not take that worthy on trust, but reads the *Chronicle of Jocelin of Brakelonde*, will find that the Abbot was an unscrupulous ruffian, combining the vices of a tyrannous landlord with those of a pettifogging attorney. Carlyle's other heroes are at least equally objectionable. Cromwell's massacres in Ireland move him to the comment: "But in Oliver's time, as I say, there was still belief in the Judgements of God; in Oliver's time, there was yet no distracted jargon of 'abolishing Capital Punishments,' of Jean-Jacques Philanthropy, and universal rose-water in this world still so full of sin . . . Only in late decadent generations . . . can such indiscriminate mashing-up of Good and Evil into one universal patent-treacle . . . take effect in our earth." Of most of his other heroes, such as Frederick the Great, Dr. Francia and Governor Eyre, all that need be said is that their one common characteristic was a thirst for blood.

Those who still think that Carlyle was in some sense more or less Liberal should read his chapter on Democracy in *Past and Present*. Most of it is occupied with praise of William the Conqueror, and with a description of the pleasant lives enjoyed by serfs in his day. Then comes a definition of liberty: "The true liberty of a man, you would say, consisted in his finding out, or being forced to find out, the right path, and to walk thereon" (p. 263). He passes on to the statement that democracy "means despair of finding any Heroes to govern you, and contentedly putting up with the want of them." The chapter ends by stating in eloquent prophetical language, that, when democracy shall have run its full course, the problem that will remain is "that of finding government by your Real-Superiors." Is there one word in all this to which Hitler would not subscribe?

Mazzini was a milder man than Carlyle, from whom he disagreed as regards the cult of heroes. Not the individual great man, but the nation, was the object of his adoration; and, while he placed Italy highest, he allowed a role to every European nation except the Irish. He believed, however, like Carlyle, that duty should be placed above happiness, above even collective happiness. He thought that God revealed to each human conscience what was right, and that all that was necessary was that everybody should obey the moral law as felt in his own heart. He never realized that different people may genuinely differ as to what the moral law enjoins, or that what he was really demanding was that others should act according to *his* revelation. He put morals above democracy, saying: "The simple vote of a majority does not constitute sovereignty, if it evidently contradicts the supreme moral precepts . . . the will of the people is sacred, when it interprets and applies the moral law; null and impotent, when it dissociates itself from the law, and only represents caprice." This is also the opinion of Mussolini.

Only one important element has since been added to the doctrines of this school, namely the pseudo-Darwinian belief in "race." (Fichte made German superiority a matter of language, not of biological heredity.) Nietzsche, who, unlike his followers, is not a nationalist or an anti-Semite, applies the doctrine only as between different individuals: he wishes the unfit to be prevented from breeding, and he hopes, by the methods of the dog-fancier, to produce a race of super-men, who shall have all power, and for whose benefit alone the rest of mankind shall exist. But subsequent writers with a similar outlook have tried to prove that all excellence has been connected with their own race. Irish professors write books to prove that Homer was an Irishman; French anthropologists give archaeological evidence that the Celts, not the Teutons, were the source of civilization in Northern Europe; Houston Chamberlain argues at length that Dante was a German and Christ was not a Jew. Emphasis upon race has been universal among Anglo-Indians, from whom imperialist England caught the infection through the medium of Rudyard Kipling. But the anti-Semite element has never been prominent in England, although an Englishman, Houston Chamberlain, was mainly responsible for giving it a sham historical basis in Germany, where it had persisted ever since the Middle Ages.

About race, if politics were not involved it would be enough to say that nothing politically important is known. It may be taken as probable that there are genetic mental differences between races; but it is certain that we do not yet know what these differences are. In an adult man, the effects of environment mask those of heredity. Moreover, the racial differences among different Europeans are less definite than those between white, yellow, and black men; there are no well-marked physical characteristics by which members of different modern European nations can be certainly known apart, since all have resulted from a mixture of different stocks. When it comes to mental superiority, every civilized nation can make out a plausible claim, which proves that all the claims are equally invalid. It is *possible* that the Jews are inferior to the Germans, but it is just as possible that the Germans are inferior to the Jews. The whole business of introducing pseudo-Darwinian jargon in such a question is utterly unscientific. Whatever we may come to know hereafter, we have not at present any good ground for wishing to encourage one race at the expense of another.

The whole movement, from Fichte onwards, is a method of bolstering up self-esteem and lust for power by means of beliefs which have nothing in their favour except that they are flattering. Fichte needed a doctrine which would make him feel superior to Napoleon; Carlyle and Nietzsche had infirmities for which they sought compensation in the world of imagination; British imperialism of Rudyard Kipling's epoch was due to shame at having lost industrial supremacy; and the Hitlerite madness of our time is a mantle of myth in which the German ego keeps itself warm against cold blasts of Versailles. No man thinks sanely when his self-esteem has suffered a mortal wound, and those who deliberately humiliate a nation have only themselves to thank if it becomes a nation of lunatics.

This brings me to the reasons which have produced the wide acceptance of the irrational and even antirational doctrine that we have been considering. There are at most times all sorts of doctrines being preached by all sorts of prophets, but those which become popular must make some special appeal to the moods produced by the circumstances of the time. Now the characteristic doctrines of modern irrationalists, as we have seen, are: emphasis on *will* as opposed to thought and feeling; glorification of power; belief in intuitional "positing" of propositions as opposed to observational and inductive testing. This state of mind is the natural reaction of those who have the habit of controlling modern mechanisms such as aeroplanes, and also of those who have less power than formerly, but are unable to find any rational ground for the restoration of their former preponderance. Industrialism and the war, while giving the habit of mechanical power, caused a great shift of economic and political power, and therefore left large groups in the mood for pragmatic self-assertion. Hence the growth of Fascism.

Comparing the world of 1920 with that of 1820, we find that there had been an increase of power on the part of: large industrialists, wage-earners, women and heretics. (By "heretics" I mean those whose religion was not that of the Government of their country.) Correlatively, there had been a loss of power on the part of: monarchs, aristocracies, ecclesiastics, the lower middle classes, and males as opposed to females. The large industrialists, though stronger than at any previous period, felt themselves insecure owing to the threat of Socialism, and more particularly from fear of Moscow. The war interests—generals, admirals, aviators, and armament firms—were in the like case: strong at the moment, but menaced by a pestilential crew of Bolsheviks and pacifists. The sections already defeated —the kings and nobles, the small shopkeepers, the men who from temperament were opponents of religious toleration, and the men who regretted the days of masculine domination over women—seemed to be definitely down and out; economic and cultural developments, it was thought, had left no place for them in the modern world. Naturally they were discontented, and collectively they were numerous. The Nietzschean philosophy was psychologically adapted to their mental needs, and, cleverly, the industrialists and militarists made use of it to weld the defeated sections into a party which should support a medievalist reaction in everything except industry and war. In regard to industry and war, there was to be everything modern in the way of technique, but not the sharing out of power and the effort after peace that made the Socialists dangerous to the existing magnates.

Thus the irrational elements in the Nazi philosophy are due, politically speaking, to the need of enlisting the support of sections which have no longer any *raison d'être*, while the comparatively sane elements are due to the industrialists and militarists. The former elements are "irrational" because it is scarcely possible that the small shopkeepers, for example, should realize their hopes, and fantastic beliefs are their only refuge from despair; *per contra*, the hopes of industrialists and militarists might be realized by means of Fascism, but hardly in any other way. The fact that their hopes can only be achieved through the ruin of civilization does not make them irrational, but only Satanic. These men form intellectually the best, and morally the worst, element in the movement; the rest, dazzled by the vision of glory, heroism, and self-sacrifice, have become blind to their serious interests, and in a blaze of emotion have allowed themselves to be used for purposes not their own. This is the psycho-pathology of Nazidom.

I have spoken of the industrialists and militarists who support Fascism as sane, but their sanity is only comparative. Thyssen believes that, by means of the Nazi movement, he can both kill Socialism and immensely increase his market. There seems, however, no more reason to think him right than there was to think that his predecessors were right in 1914. It is necessary for him to stir up German self-confidence and nationalist feeling to a dangerous degree, and unsuccessful war is the most probable outcome. Even great initial successes would not bring ultimate victory; now, as twenty years ago, the German Government forgets America.

There is one very important element which is on the whole against the Nazis although it might have been expected to support reaction—I mean, organized religion. The philosophy of the movement which culminates in the Nazis is, in a sense, a logical development of Protestantism. The morality of Fichte and

Carlyle is Calvinistic, and Mazzini, who was in lifelong opposition to Rome, had a thoroughly Lutheran belief in the infallibility of the individual conscience. Nietzsche believed passionately in the worth of the individual, and considered that the hero should not submit to authority; in this he was developing the Protestant spirit of revolt. It might have been expected that the Protestant Churches would welcome the Nazi movement, and to a certain extent they did so. But in all those elements which Protestantism shared with Catholicism, it found itself opposed by the new philosophy. Nietzsche is emphatically anti-Christian, and Houston Chamberlain gives an impression that Christianity was a degraded superstition which grew up among the mongrel cosmopolitans of the Levant. The rejection of humility, of love of one's neighbour, and of the rights of the meek, is contrary to Gospel teaching; and anti-Semitism, when it is theoretical as well as practical, is not easily reconciled with a religion of Jewish origin. For these reasons, Nazidom and Christianity have difficulty in making friends, and it is not impossible that their antagonism may bring about the downfall of the Nazis.

There is another reason why the modern cult of unreason, whether in Germany or elsewhere, is incompatible with any traditional form of Christianity. Inspired by Judaism, Christianity adopted the notion of Truth, with the correlative virtue of Faith. The notion and the virtue survived in "honest doubt," as all the Christian virtues remained among Victorian free-thinkers. But gradually the influence of scepticism and advertising made it seem hopeless to discover truth, but very profitable to assert falsehood. Intellectual probity was thus destroyed. Hitler, explaining the Nazi programme, says:—

"The national State will look upon science as a means for increasing national pride. Not only world-history, but also the history of civilization, must be taught from this point of view. The inventor should appear great, not merely as an inventor, but even more so as a fellow-countryman. Admiration of any great deed must be combined with pride because the fortunate doer of it is a member of our own nation. We must extract the greatest from the mass of great names in German history and place them before the youth in so impressive a fashion that they may become the pillars of an unshakable nationalist sentiment."

The conception of science as a pursuit of truth has so entirely disappeared from Hitler's mind that he does not even argue against it. As we know, the theory of relativity has come to be thought bad because it was invented by a Jew. The Inquisition rejected Galileo's doctrine because it considered it untrue; but Hitler accepts or rejects doctrines on political grounds, without bringing in the notion of truth or falsehood. Poor William James, who invented this point of view, would be horrified at the use which is made of it; but when once the conception of objective truth is abandoned, it is clear that the question "what shall I believe?" is one to be settled, as I wrote in 1907, by "the appeal to force and the arbitrament of the big battalions," not by the methods of either theology or science. States whose policy is based upon the revolt against reason must therefore find themselves in conflict, not only with learning, but also with the Churches wherever any genuine Christianity survives.

An important element in the causation of the revolt against reason is that many able and energetic men have no outlet for their love of power, and therefore become subversive. Small States, formerly, gave more men political power, and small businesses gave more men economic power. Consider the huge population that sleeps in suburbs and works in great cities. Coming into London by train, one passes through great regions of small villas, inhabited by families which feel no solidarity with the working class; the man of the family has no part in local affairs, since he is absent all day submitting to the orders of his employers; his only outlet for initiative is the cultivation of his back garden at the week-end. Politically, he is envious of all that is done for the working classes, but, though he feels poor, snobbery prevents him from adopting the methods of Socialism and trade unionism. His suburb may be as populous as many a famous city of antiquity, but its collective life is languid, and he has no time to be interested in it. To such a man, if he has enough spirit for discontent, a Fascist movement may well appear as a deliverance.

The decay of reason in politics is a product of two factors: on the one hand, there are classes and types of individuals to whom the world as it is offers no scope, but who see no hope in Socialism because they are not wage-earners; on the other hand, there are able and powerful men whose interests are opposed to those of the community at large, and who, therefore, can best retain their influence by promoting various kinds of hysteria. Anti-Communism, fear of foreign armaments, and hatred of foreign competition, are the most important bogeys. I do not mean that no rational man could feel these sentiments; I mean that they are used in a way to preclude intelligent consideration of practical issues. The two things the world needs most are Socialism and peace, but both are contrary to the interests of the most powerful men of our time. It is not difficult to make the steps leading up to them *appear* contrary to the interests of large sections of the population, and the easiest way of doing this is to generate mass hysteria. The greater the danger of Socialism and peace, the more Governments will debauch the mental life of their subjects; and the greater the economic hardships of the present, the more willing the sufferers will be to be seduced from intellectual sobriety in favour of some delusive will-o'-the-wisp.

The fever of nationalism which has been increasing ever since 1848 is one form of the cult of unreason. The idea of one universal truth has been abandoned: there is English truth, French truth, German truth, Montenegran truth, and truth for the principality of Monaco. Similarly there is truth for the wage-earner and truth for the capitalist. Between these different "truths," if rational persuasion is despaired of, the only possible decision is by means of war and rivalry in propagandist insanity. Until the deep conflicts of nations and classes which infect our world have been resolved, it is hardly to be expected that mankind will return to a rational habit of mind. The difficulty is that, so long as unreason prevails, a solution of our troubles can only be reached by chance; for while reason, being impersonal, makes universal co-operation possible, unreason, since it represents private passions, makes strife inevitable. It is for this reason that rationality, in the sense of an appeal to a universal and impersonal standard of truth, is of supreme importance to the well-being of the human species, not only in ages in which it easily prevails, but also, and even more, in those less fortunate times in which it is despised and rejected as the vain dream of men who lack the vitality to kill where they cannot agree.

STOICISM AND MENTAL HEALTH

By means of modern psychology, many educational problems which were formerly tackled (very unsuccessfully) by sheer moral discipline are now solved by more indirect but also more scientific methods. There is, perhaps, a tendency, especially among the less well-informed devotees of psycho-analysis, to think that there is no longer any need of stoic self-command. I do not hold this view, and in the present essay I wish to consider some of the situations which make it necessary, and some of the methods by which it can be created in young people; also some of the dangers to be avoided in creating it.

Let us begin at once with the most difficult and most essential of the problems that call for stoicism: I mean, Death. There are various ways of attempting to cope with the fear of death. We may try to ignore it; we may never mention it, and always try to turn our thoughts in another direction when we find ourselves dwelling on it. This is the method of the butterfly people in Wells's *Time Machine.* Or we may adopt the exactly opposite course, and meditate continually concerning the brevity of human life, in the hope that familiarity will breed contempt; this was the course adopted by Charles V in his cloister after his abdication. There was a Fellow of a Cambridge College who even went so far as to sleep with his coffin in the room, and who used to go out on to the College lawns with a spade to cut worms in two, saying as he did so: "Yah! you haven't got me yet." There is a third course, which has been very widely adopted, and that is, to persuade oneself and others that death is not death, but the gateway to a new and better life. These three methods, mingled in varying proportions, cover most people's accommodations to the uncomfortable fact that we die.

To each of these methods, however, there are objections. The attempt to avoid thinking about an emotionally interesting subject, as the Freudians have pointed out in connection with sex, is sure to be unsuccessful, and to lead to various kinds of undesirable contortions. Now it may, of course, be possible, in the life of a child, to ward off knowledge of death, in any poignant form, throughout the earlier years. Whether this happens or not, is a matter of luck. If a parent or brother or sister dies, there is nothing to be done to prevent a child from acquiring an emotional awareness of death. Even if, by luck, the fact of death does not become vivid to a child in early years, it must do so sooner or later; and in those who are quite unprepared, there is likely to be a serious loss of balance when this occurs. We must therefore seek to establish some attitude towards death other than that of merely ignoring it.

The practice of brooding continually on death is at least equally harmful. It is a mistake to think too exclusively about any one subject, more particularly when our thinking cannot issue in action. We can, of course, act so as to postpone our own death, and within limits every normal person does so. But we cannot prevent ourselves from dying ultimately; this is, therefore, a profitless subject of meditation. Moreover, it tends to diminish a man's interest in other people and events, and it is only objective interests that can preserve mental health. Fear of death makes a man feel himself the slave of external forces, and from a slave mentality no good result can follow. If, by meditation, a man could genuinely cure himself of the fear of death, he would cease to meditate on the subject; so long as it absorbs his thoughts, that proves that he has not ceased to fear it. This method, therefore, is no better than the other.

The belief that death is a gateway to a better life ought, logically, to prevent men from feeling any fear of death. Fortunately for the medical profession, it does not in fact have this effect, except in a few rare instances. One does not find that believers in a future life are less afraid of illness or more courageous in battle than those who think that death ends all. The late F. W. H. Myers used to tell how he asked a man at a dinner table what he thought would happen to him when he died. The man tried to ignore the question, but, on being pressed, replied: "Oh well, I suppose I shall inherit eternal bliss, but I wish you wouldn't talk about such unpleasant subjects." The reason for this apparent inconsistency is, of course, that religious belief, in most people, exists only in the region of conscious thought, and has not succeeded in modifying unconscious mechanisms. If the fear of death is to be coped with successfully, it must be by some method which affects behaviour as a whole, not only that part of behaviour that is commonly called conscious thought. In a few instances, religious belief can effect this, but not in the majority of mankind. Apart from behaviouristic reasons, there are two other sources of this failure: one is a certain doubt which persists in spite of fervent professions, and shows itself in the form of anger with sceptics; the other is the fact that believers in a future life tend to emphasize, rather than minimize, the horror that would attach to death if their beliefs were unfounded, and so to increase fear in those who do not feel absolute certainty.

What, then, shall we do with young people to adapt them to a world in which death exists? We have to achieve three objects, which are very difficult to combine. (1) We must give them no feeling that death is a subject about which we do not wish to speak or to encourage them to think. If we give them such a feeling, they will conclude that there is an interesting mystery, and will think all the more. On this point, the familiar modern position on sex education is applicable. (2) We must nevertheless so act as to prevent them, if we can, from thinking much or often on the matter of death; there is the same kind of objection to such absorption as to absorption in pornography, namely that it diminishes efficiency, prevents all-round development, and leads to conduct which is unsatisfactory both to the person concerned and to others. (3) We must not hope to create in anyone a satisfactory attitude on the subject of death by means of conscious thought alone; more particularly, no good is done by beliefs intended to show that death is less terrible than it otherwise would be, when (as is usual) such beliefs do not penetrate below the level of consciousness.

To give effect to these various objects, we shall have to adopt somewhat different methods according to the experience of the child or young person. If no one closely connected with the child dies, it is fairly easy to secure an acceptance of death as a common fact, of no great emotional interest. So long as death is abstract and impersonal, it should be mentioned in a matter-of-fact voice, not as something terrible. If the child asks, "Shall I die?" one should say, "Yes, but probably not for a long time." It is important to prevent any sense of mystery about death. It should be brought into the same category with the wearing out of toys. But it is certainly desirable, if possible, to make it seem very distant while children are young.

When someone of importance to the child dies, the matter is different. Suppose, for example, the child loses a brother. The parents are unhappy, and although they may not wish the child to know *how* unhappy they are, it is right and necessary that he should perceive *something* of what they suffer. Natural affection is of very great importance, and the child should feel that his elders feel it. Moreover, if, by superhuman efforts, they conceal their sorrow from the child, he may think: "They wouldn't mind if I died." Such a thought might start all kinds of morbid developments. Therefore, although the shock of such an occurrence is harmful when it occurs during late childhood (in early childhood it will not be felt much), yet, if it occurs, we must not minimize it too much. The subject must be neither avoided nor dwelt upon; what is possible without any too obvious intention, must be done to create fresh interests, and above all fresh affections. I think that very intense affection for some one individual, in a child, is not infrequently a mark of something amiss. Such affection may arise towards one parent if the other parent is unkind, or towards a teacher if both parents are unkind. It is generally a product of fear: the object of affection is the only person who gives a sense of safety. Affection of this kind, in childhood, is not wholesome. Where it exists the death of the person loved may shatter the child's life. Even if all seems well outwardly, every subsequent love will be filled with terror. Husband (or wife) and children will be plagued by undue solicitude, and will be thought heartless when they are merely living their own lives. A parent ought not, therefore, to feel pleased at being the object of this kind of affection. If the child has a generally friendly environment and is happy, he will, without much trouble, get over the pain of any one loss that may happen to him. The impulse to life and hope ought to be sufficient, provided the normal opportunities for growth and happiness exist.

During adolescence, however, there is need of something more positive in the way of an attitude towards death, if adult life is to be satisfactory. The adult should think little about death, either his own or that of people whom he loves, not because he deliberately turns his thoughts to other things, for that is a useless exercise which never really succeeds, but because of the multiplicity of his interests and activities. When he does think of death, it is best to think with a certain stoicism, deliberately and calmly, not attempting to minimize its importance, but feeling a certain pride in rising above it. The principle is the same as in the case of any other terror: resolute contemplation of the terrifying object is the only possible treatment. One must say to oneself: "Well, yes, that might happen, but what of it?" People achieve this in such a case as death in battle, because they are then firmly persuaded of the importance of the cause to which they have given their life, or the life of someone dear to them. Something of this way of feeling is desirable at all times. At all times, a man should feel that there are matters of importance for which he lives, and that his death, or the death of wife or child, does not put an end to all that interests him in the world. If this attitude is to be genuine and profound in adult life, it is necessary that, in adolescence, a youth should be fired with generous enthusiasms, and that he should build his life and career about them. Adolescence is the period of generosity, and it should be utilized for the formation of generous habits. This can be achieved by the influence of the father or of the teacher. In a better community, the mother would often be the one to do it, but as a rule, at present, the lives of women are such as to make their outlook too personal and not sufficiently intellectual for what I have in mind. For the same reason, adolescents (female as well as male) ought, as a rule, to have men among their teachers, until a new generation of women has grown up which is more impersonal in its interests.

The place of stoicism in life has, perhaps, been somewhat underestimated in recent times, particularly by progressive educationists. When misfortune threatens, there are two ways of dealing with the situation: we may try to avoid the misfortune, or we may decide that we will meet it with fortitude. The former method is admirable where it is available without cowardice; but the latter is necessary, sooner or later, for anyone who is not prepared to be the slave of fear. This attitude constitutes stoicism. The great difficulty, for an educator, is that the instilling of stoicism in the young affords an outlet for sadism. In the past, ideas of discipline were so fierce that education became a channel for impulses of cruelty. Is it possible to give the necessary minimum of discipline without developing a pleasure in making the child suffer? Old-fashioned people will, of course, deny that they feel any such pleasure. Everyone knows the story of the boy whose father, while administering the cane, said: "My boy, this hurts me more than it does you"; to which the boy replied: "Then, father, will you let me do it to you instead?" Samuel Butler, in *The Way of All Flesh*, has depicted the sadistic pleasures of stern parents in a way which is convincing to any student of modern psychology. What, then, are we to do about it?

The fear of death is only one of many that are best dealt with by stoicism. There is the fear of poverty, the fear of physical pain, the fear of childbirth which is common among well-to-do women. All such fears are weakening and more or less contemptible. But if we take the line that people ought not to mind such things, we shall tend also to take the line that nothing need be done to mitigate evils. For a long time, it was thought that women ought not to have anaesthetics in childbirth; in Japan, this opinion persists to the present day. Male doctors held that anaesthetics would be harmful; there was no reason for this view, which was doubtless due to unconscious sadism. But the more the pains of childbirth have been mitigated, the less willing rich women have become to endure them: their courage had diminished faster than the need of it. Evidently there must be a balance. It is impossible to make the whole of life soft and pleasant, and therefore human beings must be capable of an attitude suitable to the unpleasant portions; but we must try to bring this about with as little encouragement to cruelty as possible.

Whoever has to deal with young children soon learns

that too much sympathy is a mistake. Too little sympathy is, of course, a worse mistake, but in this, as in everything else, each extreme is bad. A child that invariably receives sympathy will continue to cry over every tiny mishap; the ordinary self-control of the average adult is only achieved through knowledge that no sympathy will be won by making a fuss. Children readily understand that an adult who is sometimes a little stern is best for them; their instinct tells them whether they are loved or not, and from those whom they feel to be affectionate they will put up with whatever strictness results from genuine desire for their proper development. Thus in theory the solution is simple: let educators be inspired by wise love, and they will do the right thing. In fact, however, the matter is more complicated. Fatigue, vexation, worry, impatience, beset the parent or teacher, and it is dangerous to have an educational theory which allows the adult to vent these feelings upon the child for the sake of his ultimate welfare. Nevertheless, if the theory is true, it must be accepted, and the dangers must be brought before the consciousness of the parent or teacher, so that everything possible may be done to guard against them.

We can now sum up the conclusions suggested by the foregoing discussion. In regard to the painful hazards of life, knowledge of them, on the part of children, should be neither avoided nor obtruded; it should come when circumstances make it unavoidable. Painful things, when they have to be mentioned, should be treated truthfully and unemotionally, except when a death occurs in the family, in which case it would be unnatural to conceal sorrow. The adults should display in their own conduct a certain gay courage, which the young will unconsciously acquire from their example. In adolescence, large impersonal interests should be set before the young, and education should be so conducted as to give them the idea (by suggestion, not by explicit exhortation) of living for purposes outside themselves. They should be taught to endure misfortune, when it comes, by remembering that there are still things to live for; but they should not brood on possible misfortunes, even for the purpose of being prepared to meet them. Those whose business it is to deal with the young must keep a close watch upon themselves to see that they do not derive a sadistic pleasure from the necessary element of discipline in education; the motive for discipline must always be the development of character or intelligence. For the intellect, also, requires discipline, without which accuracy will never be achieved. But the discipline of the intellect is a different topic, and lies outside the scope of this essay.

I have only one more word to say, and that is, that discipline is best when it springs from an inner impulse. In order that this may be possible, it is necessary that the child or adolescent should feel the ambition to achieve something difficult, and should be willing to make efforts to that end. Such ambition is usually suggested by some person in the environment; thus even self-discipline depends, in the end, upon an educational stimulus.

MODERN HOMOGENEITY

The European traveller in America—at least if I may judge by myself—is struck by two peculiarities: first the extreme similarity of outlook in all parts of the United States (except the old South), and secondly the passionate desire of each locality to prove that it is peculiar and different from every other. The second of these is, of course, caused by the first. Every place wishes to have a reason for local pride, and therefore cherishes whatever is distinctive in the way of geography or history or tradition. The greater the uniformity that in fact exists, the more eager becomes the search for differences that may mitigate it. The old South is in fact quite unlike the rest of America, so unlike that one feels as if one had arrived in a different country. It is agricultural, aristocratic, and retrospective, whereas the rest of America is industrial, democratic, and prospective. When I say that America outside the old South is industrial, I am thinking even of those parts that are devoted almost wholly to agriculture, for the mentality of the American agriculturist is industrial. He uses much modern machinery; he is intimately dependent upon the railway and the telephone; he is very conscious of the distant markets to which his products are sent; he is in fact a capitalist who might just as well be in some other business. A peasant, as he exists in Europe and Asia, is practically unknown in the United States. This is an immense boon to America, and per-

haps its most important superiority as compared to the
Old World, for the peasant everywhere is cruel, avari-
cious, conservative, and inefficient. I have seen orange
groves in Sicily and orange groves in California; the
contrast represents a period of about two thousand
years. Orange groves in Sicily are remote from trains
and ships; the trees are old and gnarled and beautiful;
the methods are those of classical antiquity. The men
are ignorant and semi-savage, mongrel descendants of
Roman slaves and Arab invaders; what they lack in
intelligence towards trees they make up for by cruelty
to animals. With moral degradation and economic in-
competence goes an instinctive sense of beauty which
is perpetually reminding one of Theocritus and the
myth about the Garden of the Hesperides. In a Cali-
fornian orange grove the Garden of the Hesperides
seems very remote. The trees are all exactly alike, carefully tended and at the right distance apart. The
oranges, it is true, are not all exactly of the same size,
but careful machinery sorts them so that automatically
all those in one box are exactly similar. They travel
along with suitable things being done to them by suitable machines at suitable points until they enter a
suitable refrigerator car in which they travel to a suitable market. The machine stamps the word "Sunkist"
upon them, but otherwise there is nothing to suggest
that nature has any part in their production. Even the
climate is artificial, for when there would otherwise
be frost, the orange grove is kept artificially warm by
a pall of smoke. The men engaged in agriculture of
this kind do not feel themselves, like the agriculturists
of former times, the patient servants of natural forces;
on the contrary, they feel themselves the masters, and
able to bend natural forces to their will. There is therefore not the same difference in America as in the Old
World between the outlook of industrialists and that
of agriculturists. The important part of the environment in America is the human part; by comparison the
non-human part sinks into insignificance. I was con-

stantly assured in Southern California that the climate
turned people into lotus eaters, but I confess I saw no
evidence of this. They seemed to me exactly like the
people in Minneapolis or Winnipeg, although climate,
scenery, and natural conditions were as different as
possible in the two regions. When one considers the
difference between a Norwegian and a Sicilian, and
compares it with the lack of difference between a man
from (say) North Dakota and a man from Southern
California, one realizes the immense revolution in human affairs which has been brought about by man's
becoming the master instead of the slave of his physical
environment. Norway and Sicily both have ancient
traditions; they had pre-Christian religions embodying
men's reactions to the climate, and when Christianity
came it inevitably took very different forms in the
two countries. The Norwegian feared ice and snow; the
Sicilian feared lava and earthquakes. Hell was invented
in a southern climate; if it had been invented in Norway, it would have been cold. But neither in North
Dakota nor in Southern California is Hell a climatic
condition: in both it is a stringency on the money
market. This illustrates the unimportance of climate
in modern life.

America is a man-made world; moreover it is a world
which man has made by means of machinery. I am
thinking not only of the physical environment, but also
and quite as much of thoughts and emotions. Consider
a really stirring murder: the murderer, it is true, may be
primitive in his methods, but those who spread the
knowledge of his deed do so by means of all the latest
resources of science. Not only in the great cities, but
in lonely farms on the prairie and in mining camps in
the Rockies, the radio disseminates all the latest information, so that half the topics of conversation on
a given day are the same in every household throughout the country. As I was crossing the plains in the
train, endeavouring not to hear a loud-speaker bellow-
ing advertisements of soap, an old farmer came up to

me with a beaming face and said, "Wherever you go nowadays you can't get away from civilization." Alas! How true! I was endeavouring to read Virginia Woolf, but the advertisements won the day.

Uniformity in the physical apparatus of life would be no grave matter, but uniformity in matters of thought and opinion is much more dangerous. It is, however, a quite inevitable result of modern inventions. Production is cheaper when it is unified and on a large scale than when it is divided into a number of small units. This applies quite as much to the production of opinions as to the production of pins. The principal sources of opinion in the present day are the schools, the Churches, the Press, the cinema, and the radio. The teaching in the elementary schools must inevitably become more and more standardized as more use is made of apparatus. It may, I think, be assumed that both the cinema and the radio will play a rapidly increasing part in school education in the near future. This will mean that the lessons will be produced at a centre and will be precisely the same wherever the material prepared at this centre is used. Some Churches, I am told, send out every week a model sermon to all the less educated of their clergy, who, if they are governed by the ordinary laws of human nature, are no doubt grateful for being saved the trouble of composing a sermon of their own. This model sermon, of course, deals with some burning topic of the moment, and aims at arousing a given mass emotion throughout the length and breadth of the land. The same thing applies in a higher degree to the Press, which receives everywhere the same telegraphic news and is syndicated on a large scale. Reviews of my books, I find, are, except in the best newspapers, verbally the same from New York to San Francisco, and from Maine to Texas, except that they become shorter as one travels from the north-east to the south-west.

Perhaps the greatest of all forces for uniformity in

the modern world is the cinema, since its influence is not confined to America but penetrates to all parts of the world, except the Soviet Union, which, however, has its own different uniformity. The cinema embodies, broadly speaking, Hollywood's opinion of what is liked in the Middle West. Our emotions in regard to love and marriage, birth and death, are becoming standardized according to this recipe. To the young of all lands Hollywood represents the last word in modernity, displaying both the pleasures of the rich and the methods to be adopted for acquiring riches. I suppose the talkies will lead before long to the adoption of a universal language, which will be that of Hollywood.

It is not only among the comparatively ignorant that there is uniformity in America. The same thing applies, though in a slightly less degree, to culture. I visited book shops in every part of the country, and found everywhere the same best-sellers prominently displayed. So far as I could judge, the cultured ladies of America buy every year about a dozen books, the same dozen everywhere. To an author this is a very satisfactory state of affairs, provided he is one of the dozen. But it certainly does mark a difference from Europe, where there are many books with small sales rather than a few with large sales.

It must not be supposed that the tendency towards uniformity is either wholly good or wholly bad. It has great advantages and also great disadvantages: its chief advantage is, of course, that it produces a population capable of peaceable co-operation; its great disadvantage is that it produces a population prone to persecution of minorities. This latter defect is probably temporary, since it may be assumed that before long there will be no minorities. A great deal depends, of course, on how the uniformity is achieved. Take, for example, what the schools do to southern Italians. Southern Italians have been distinguished throughout history for murder, graft, and aesthetic sensibility. The Public Schools effectively cure them of the last of these three,

and to that extent assimilate them to the native American population, but in regard to the other two distinctive qualities, I gather that the success of the schools is
less marked. This illustrates one of the dangers of uniformity as an aim: good qualities are easier to destroy
than bad ones, and therefore uniformity is most easily
achieved by lowering all standards. It is, of course, clear
that a country with a large foreign population must
endeavour, through its schools, to assimilate the children of immigrants, and therefore a certain degree of
Americanization is inevitable. It is, however, unfortu-
nate that such a large part of this process should be
effected by means of a somewhat blatant nationalism.
America is already the strongest country in the world,
and its preponderance is continually increasing. This
fact naturally inspires fear in Europe, and the fear is
increased by everything suggesting militant nationalism.
It may be the destiny of America to teach political
good sense to Europe, but I am afraid that the pupil
is sure to prove refractory.

With the tendency towards uniformity in America
there goes, as it seems to me, a mistaken conception
of democracy. It seems to be generally held in the
United States that democracy requires all men to be
alike, and that, if a man is in any way different from
another, he is "setting himself up" as superior to that
other. France is quite as democratic as America, and
yet this idea does not exist in France. The doctor, the
lawyer, the priest, the public official are all different
types in France; each profession has its own traditions
and its own standards, although it does not set up to be
superior to other professions. In America all professional men are assimilated in type to the business man.
It is as though one should decree that an orchestra
should consist only of violins. There does not seem to
be an adequate understanding of the fact that society
should be a pattern or an organism, in which different
organs play different parts. Imagine the eye and the
ear quarrelling as to whether it is better to see or to

hear, and deciding that each would do neither since neither could do both. This, it seems to me, would be democracy as understood in America. There is a strange envy of any kind of excellence which cannot be universal except, of course, in the sphere of athletics and sport, where aristocracy is enthusiastically acclaimed. It seems that the average American is more capable of humility in regard to his muscles than in regard to his brains; perhaps this is because his admiration for muscle is more profound and genuine than his admiration of brains. The flood of popular scientific books in America is inspired partly, though of course not wholly, by the unwillingness to admit that there is anything in science which only experts can understand. The idea that a special training may be necessary to understand, say, the theory of relativity, causes a sort of irritation, although nobody is irritated by the fact that a special training is necessary in order to be a first-rate football player.

Achieved eminence is perhaps more admired in America than in any other country, and yet the road to certain kinds of eminence is made very difficult for the young, because people are intolerant of any eccentricity or anything that could be called "setting one's self up," provided the person concerned is not already labelled "eminent." Consequently many of the finished types that are most admired are difficult to produce at home and have to be imported from Europe. This fact is bound up with standardization and uniformity. Exceptional merit, especially in artistic directions, is bound to meet with great obstacles in youth so long as everybody is expected to conform outwardly to a pattern set by the successful executive.

Standardization, though it may have disadvantages for the exceptional individual, probably increases the happiness of the average man, since he can utter his thoughts with a certainty that they will be like the thoughts of his hearer. Moreover it promotes national cohesion, and makes politics less bitter and violent than where more marked differences exist. I do not think it is possible to strike a balance of gains and losses, but I think the standardization which now exists in America is likely to exist throughout Europe as the world becomes more mechanized. Europeans, therefore, who find fault with America on this account should realize that they are finding fault with the future of their own countries, and are setting themselves against an inevitable and universal trend in civilization. Undoubtedly internationalism will become easier as the differences between nations diminish, and if once internationalism were established, social cohesion would become of enormous importance for preserving internal peace. There is a certain risk, which cannot be denied, of an immobility analogous to that of the late Roman Empire. But as against this, we may set the revolutionary forces of modern science and modern technique. Short of a universal intellectual decay, these forces, which are a new feature in the modern world, will make immobility impossible, and prevent that kind of stagnation which has overtaken great empires in the past. Arguments from history are dangerous to apply to the present and the future, because of the complete change that science has introduced. I see therefore no reason for undue pessimism, however standardization may offend the tastes of those who are unaccustomed to it.

MEN *versus* INSECTS

Amid wars and rumours of wars, while "disarmament" proposals and non-aggression pacts threaten the human race with unprecedented disaster, another conflict, perhaps even more important, is receiving much less notice than it deserves—I mean the conflict between men and insects.

We are accustomed to being the Lords of Creation; we no longer have occasion, like the cave men, to fear lions and tigers, mammoths and wild boars. Except against each other, we feel ourselves safe. But while big animals no longer threaten our existence, it is otherwise with small animals. Once before in the history of life on this planet, large animals gave place to small ones. For many ages dinosaurs ranged unconcerned through swamp and forest, fearing nothing but each other, not doubting the absoluteness of their empire. But they disappeared, to give place to tiny mammals—mice, small hedgehogs, miniature horses no bigger than rats, and such-like. Why the dinosaurs died out is not known, but it is supposed to be because they had minute brains and devoted themselves to the growth of weapons of offence in the shape of numerous horns. However that may be, it was not through their line that life developed.

The mammals, having become supreme, proceeded to grow big. But the biggest on land, the mammoth, is

122

extinct, and the other large animals have grown rare, except man and those that he has domesticated. Man, by his intelligence, has succeeded in finding nourishment for a large population, in spite of his size. He is safe, except from the little creatures—the insects and the micro-organisms.

Insects have an initial advantage in their numbers. A small wood may easily contain as many ants as there are human beings in the whole world. They have another advantage in the fact that they eat our food before it is ripe for us. Many noxious insects which used to live only in some one comparatively small region have been unintentionally transported by man to new environments where they have done immense damage. Travel and trade are useful to insects as well as to micro-organisms. Yellow fever formerly existed only in West Africa, but was carried to the Western hemisphere by the slave trade. Now, owing to the opening up of Africa, it is gradually travelling eastward across that continent. When it reaches the east coast it will become almost impossible to keep it out of India and China, where it may be expected to halve the population. Sleeping sickness is an even more deadly African disease which is gradually spreading.

Fortunately science has discovered ways by which insect pests can be kept under. Most of them are liable to parasites which kill so many that the survivors cease to be a serious problem, and entomologists are engaged in studying and breeding such parasites. Official reports of their activities are fascinating; they are full of such sentences as: "He proceeded to Brazil, at the request of the planters of Trinidad, to search for the natural enemies of the sugar-cane Froghopper." One would say that the sugar-cane Froghopper would have little chance in this contest. Unfortunately, so long as war continues, all scientific knowledge is double-edged. For example, Professor Fritz Haber, who has just died, invented a process for the fixation of nitrogen. He intended it to increase the fertility of the soil, but the

German Government used it for the manufacture of high explosives, and has recently exiled him for preferring manure to bombs. In the next great war, the scientists on either side will let loose pests on the crops of the other side, and it may prove scarcely possible to destroy the pests when peace comes. The more we know, the more harm we can do each other. If human beings, in their rage against each other, invoke the aid of insects and microorganisms, as they certainly will do if there is another big war, it is by no means unlikely that the insects will remain the sole ultimate victors. Perhaps, from a cosmic point of view, this is not to be regretted; but as a human being I cannot help heaving a sigh over my own species.

ON COMETS

If I were a comet, I should consider the men of our present age a degenerate breed.

In former times, the respect for comets was universal and profound. One of them foreshadowed the death of Caesar; another was regarded as indicating the approaching death of the Emperor Vespasian. He himself was a strong-minded man, and maintained that the comet must have some other significance, since it was hairy and he was bald; but there were few who shared this extreme of Rationalism. The Venerable Bede said that "comets portend revolutions of kingdoms, pestilence, war, winds, or heat." John Knox regarded comets as evidences of divine anger, and other Scottish Protestants thought them "a warning to the King to extirpate the Papists."

America, and especially New England, came in for a due share of cometary attention. In 1652 a comet appeared just at the moment when the eminent Mr. Cotton fell ill, and disappeared at his death. Only ten years later, the wicked inhabitants of Boston were warned by a new comet to abstain from "voluptuousness and abuse of the good creatures of God by licentiousness in drinking and fashions in apparel." Increase Mather, the eminent divine, considered that comets and eclipses had portended the deaths of Presidents of Harvard and Colonial Governors, and instructed his flock to pray to the Lord that he would not "take away stars and send comets to succeed them."

All this superstition was gradually dispelled by Halley's discovery that one comet, at least, went round the sun in an orderly ellipse, just like a sensible planet, and by Newton's proof that comets obey the law of gravitation. For some time, Professors in the more old-fashioned universities were forbidden to mention these discoveries, but in the long run the truth could not be concealed.

In our day, it is difficult to imagine a world in which everybody, high and low, educated and uneducated, was preoccupied with comets, and filled with terror whenever one appeared. Most of us have never seen a comet. I have seen two, but they were far less impressive than I had expected them to be. The cause of the change in our attitude is not merely Rationalism, but artificial lighting. In the streets of a modern city the night sky is invisible; in rural districts, we move in cars with bright headlights. We have blotted out the heavens and only a few scientists remain aware of stars and planets, meteorites and comets. The world of our daily life is more man-made than at any previous epoch. In this there is loss as well as gain: Man, in the security of his dominion, is becoming trivial, arrogant, and a little mad. But I do not think a comet would now produce the wholesome moral effect which it produced in Boston in 1662; a stronger medicine would now be needed.